D1397193

Ginn English

Richard L. Venezky
Carol J. Fisher

Ginn and Company

EXPERTS IN THE FIELD

RICHARD L. VENEZKY is Unidel Professor of Educational Foundations, University of Delaware, Newark, Delaware. Dr. Venezky has conducted considerable research and published extensively in linguistics, reading processes, spelling, and computer sciences. He has also served as consultant on several comprehensive dictionaries and is an author on the Ginn Reading Program.

CAROL J. FISHER is Professor of Language Education at the University of Georgia at Athens and Chair of the Elementary Language Arts Committee. Dr. Fisher brings to Ginn English her practical experience of years of elementary and high school teaching as well as her professional expertise in Language Arts and early and middle childhood education. Dr. Fisher has served as Chair for the Elementary Section of the National Council of Teachers of English. She is the author of numerous professional articles and papers on children's writing and literature.

AUTHOR CONSULTANTS FOR ATYPICAL LEARNERS

ADALBERTO M. GUERRERO (Spanish-speaking learners), Tucson, Arizona; **KENNETH R. JOHNSON** (speakers of nonstandard English), Willits, California; **DEAN C. KINDIG** (disabled learners), Penfield, New York; **MARGE MARSHALL** (talented learners), Wilmington, Delaware

Teacher Reviewers: LILLA S. ARNOLD (Gr. 1), Atlanta, Georgia; **MARSHA Z. BEHRENS** (Gr. 5), Chicago, Illinois; **HOWARD R. BONNER** (Gr. 4), Houston, Texas; **ELIZABETH B. BRINCKERHOFF** (Gr. K), Cairo, New York; **JOHN J. BURGER** (Gr. 3), Mexico, New York; **HORTENSE E. BURTON** (Gr. 6), Haverhill, Massachusetts; **HORTENCIA FRAUSTO** (Gr. 2), San Jose, California; **KAREN JUSZCZYK** (Gr. K), Orland Park, Illinois; **CHARLES B. KITCHEN** (Gr. 6), Savannah, Georgia; **PRISCILLA M. MARTINEZ** (Gr. 1), McAllen, Texas; **VERNA MITCHELL** (Gr. 8), Matthews, North Carolina; **PHYLLIS OVERTON** (Gr. 2), Mount Pleasant, Iowa; **MARQUITA JO PEARSON** (Gr. 3), Chicago, Illinois; **ALMA PEÑA** (Gr. 4), Temple City, California; **BETTY M. SWIGGETT** (Gr. 7), Hampton, Virginia; **WILLIAM R. WATTS** (Gr. 8), Atlanta, Georgia; **PAUL G. WEISBERG** (Gr. 5), Waltham, Massachusetts

ACKNOWLEDGMENTS

Grateful acknowledgment is made to the following publishers, authors, and agents for permission to use and adapt copyrighted materials:

Harcourt Brace Jovanovich, Inc., for the poem "Curiosity" by Harry Behn. From *Windy Morning,* copyright 1953 by Harry Behn; renewed 1981 by Alice Behn Goebel, Pamela Behn Adam, Prescott Behn, and Peter Behn. Reprinted by permission of Harcourt Brace Jovanovich, Inc.

Harper & Row, Publishers, Inc., for the poem "Tiptoe" (text only) from *Dogs and Dragons, Trees and Dreams,* by Karla Kuskin. Copyright © 1958 by Karla Kuskin. By permission of Harper & Row, Publishers, Inc.

Instructor for "Skip and Waddle" by Rose Cary O'Brian. Reprinted from *Instructor,* April 1962. Copyright © 1962 by The Instructor Publications, Inc. Used by permission.

Curtis Brown, Ltd., New York, for the poems "F Is the Fighting Firetruck," "S Is the Snorting Subway," and "E Is the Escalator," all from *All around the Town* by Phyllis McGinley. Reprinted by permission of Curtis Brown, Ltd. The text copyright, 1948, by Phyllis McGinley. Copyright renewed © 1976 by Phyllis McGinley.

Levin Houston for his "Alphabet Song." Words and music © Copyright, 1979, by Levin Houston. Used by permission.

Louise M. Ihrig for "Little Duckling Tries His Voice" by Marjorie M. La Fleur. From *Child Life* Magazine, copyright 1923, 1951 by Rand McNally & Company. Used by permission of Louise M. Ihrig.

Penguin Books Ltd, London, for the adaptation of "The Tale of Peter Rabbit" by Beatrix Potter. Copyright © Frederick Warne & Company Ltd. Reprinted by permission of the publishers.

Ginn and Company for the songs "Morning Greeting" (adapted) and "A Little Boy Went Walking" (song and verses, adatpred) from *The Magic of Music—Kindergarten,* © Copyright, 1970, 1965, by Ginn and Company (Xerox Corporation). Used by permission of the publishers. Also for the adaptation of the story "Little Red Riding Hood," from *Rhymes and Stories* compiled and edited by Marion Florence Lansing, of THE OPEN ROAD LIBRARY OF JUVENILE LITERATURE, © Copyright, 1907, by Marion Florence Lansing, published by Ginn and Company (Xerox Corporation).

CONTENTS

Unit **1**
(Lessons 1–13)

Unit **2**
(Lessons 14–29)

Unit **3**
(Lessons 30–36)

COMPONENTS

STUDENT TEXTS
Grades K–8

- clear instruction
- abundant practice
- practical applications
- regular review
- unit tests
- systematic maintenance
- end-of-book handbook

TEACHER'S EDITIONS
Grades K–8

- comprehensive lesson plans
- annotated student pages
- extensive practice masters
- standardized-format tests
- help in evaluating writing
- realistic plans for individual differences

RESOURCE BOOKS
Grades 1–8

- **parent letters in English and Spanish**
- **independent writing activities**
- **help in evaluating writing**
- **diagraming practice**
- **complete testing program**
- **workbook masters**
- **five kinds of practice masters**
  Review, On–Grade, and Extension masters
  Handbook and Follow-Up activities

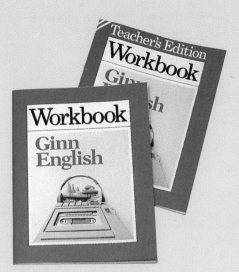
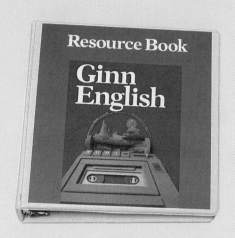

WORKBOOKS
Grades 1–8

High-interest workbooks provide additional practice for comprehensive coverage of skills. Teacher's Editions of Workbooks offer full-sized annotated student pages.

ELECTRONIC PRODUCTS THAT WORK WITH GINN ENGLISH

Computer Management System will save you the hours involved in managing a testing program. This system provides record keeping, diagnostic-prescriptive information, and a variety of reports for teachers, administrators, and parents—and you don't have to be a computer genius to use it.

Suspect Sentences offers students in Grades 6–8 a chance to test their skills against the masters of literature. Students develop a keen awareness of literary style as they have fun reading and writing.

GRADE K FEATURES

A COMPLETE PROGRAM

The Kindergarten component of **GINN ENGLISH** provides ample opportunities to develop the critical language skills needed for future success. The special features that make this possible are:

- **Oral Language Development**
- **Attention to Other Essential Skills**
- **Help for Atypical Learners**
- *Easy* and *Challenging* Additional Activities

ORAL LANGUAGE DEVELOPMENT

The three units in the Kindergarten text emphasize communication skills. Unit 1 encourages children to use their language effectively to express and receive ideas. The focus is to learn by examining what is known or seen. Unit 2 gives children opportunities to use their communication skills while examining more unfamiliar things. Unit 3 builds on a framework of communication skills established in previous units. These final lessons deal with language skills that students need for future progress.

OTHER ESSENTIAL SKILLS

Through a wide range of skill-building activities, the Kindergarten text helps develop visual and auditory discrimination skills, study skills, creative expression, and literary appreciation. The Scope and Sequence chart on pages TE xiii-xvi shows where these important skills are covered in Grade K of **GINN ENGLISH**.

The program provides you with a wide variety of learning activities that enhance the development of each child's learning and social skills.

---

2 Telling What I See

OBJECTIVES
to respond in complete sentences
to listen to and sing a song
to pantomime and imitate actions

ORAL VOCABULARY
winding   sparrow
bank   church steeple

BASIC LESSON MATERIALS
none

LESSON STEPS

- See the song "A Little Boy Went Walking," in the Resource Unit, page TE 103.

- Talk with the children about the pictures on pages 2 and 3 of their books. Tell them that the pictures show a boy walking. Ask what the boy sees. (rabbit, river with fish, birds, bridge, and church with steeple) Encourage children to respond in complete sentences. Explain any pictures that may be unfamiliar.

- Tell children that there is a song to go with the pictures. Have them listen as you sing the song, making appropriate hand/arm motions for the hopping rabbit, winding river, flying birds, the boy resting his head on his arms at the bridge, the steeple shape, and the boy going to tell his mother what he has seen. Encourage children to follow the picture as you sing the song.

This lesson is continued on the next page.

Telling What I See

ACTIVITY: listening to and singing a song   OBJECTIVE: to learn a song

2 LANGUAGE SKILLS: Telling What I See

TE 7

HELPING ATYPICAL LEARNERS

Helping Atypical Learners, a section in many lesson plans, provides specific activities for the mildly learning disabled, the bilingual Spanish-speaker, and the speaker of nonstandard English.

These specific activities for different types of learners provide you with diverse methods for meeting the individual needs for *all* students.

ADDITIONAL ACTIVITIES

Each lesson plan in the Teacher's Edition includes two types of Additional Activities. **Easy** activities will help those students who will need additional practice in the core skill. **Challenging** activities will help those children who will benefit from extending the concept.

Easy and **Challenging** activities enable you to cement and extend individual learning. Children's chances for learning and retention increase.

Lesson 2 (continued)

• Sing the song again. Encourage children to sing and move with you as they become familiar with the song.

LISTENING / SPEAKING SKILLS

Talk about how a song can tell a story. Ask children to tell the "story" this song tells. Encourage them to use complete sentences.

HELPING ATYPICAL LEARNERS

Disabled: Play *Simon Says* (Play-Off, D-2) to practice the movements in the song. Tape-record the song so that auditory learners may have many individual repetitions. (*Tape Recorder*, A-1)

Nonstandard English: If possible, tape-record the song "A Little Boy Went Walking" so that children hear and become familiar with standard pronunciation.

ADDITIONAL ACTIVITIES

Easy: On oak tag draw simple pictures of a boy, rabbit, river, fish, nest, bird, cloud, and church steeple. Children might help you cut them out. Have children take turns moving the manipulatives as the song "A Little Boy Went Walking" is sung.

Challenging: Suggest that children might want to sing "A Little Boy Went Walking" at home for their families. Or you might have them sing it for another class.

TE 8

TELLING WHAT I SEE Name _____

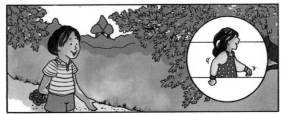

From Ginn English Program Grade K, copyrighted by Ginn and Company   LISTENING SKILLS: Singing a Song 3

STUDENT TEXT FEATURES

FROM THE KNOWN TO THE UNKNOWN

In Grade K of the **Ginn English Program,** each lesson builds on the child's experiential base to teach new skills through known vehicles. As shown in the pages reproduced here, Lesson 3 is based on nursery rhymes that are familiar to most children. These rhymes are used to teach listening skills, picture details, following directions, and cutting on lines.

FOLLOWING DIRECTIONS

Early in the Kindergarten text, children get used to following directions. In Lesson 3, for example, a picture of scissors indicates cutting direction. Different shapes and picture clues show children exactly where and how to paste each picture. Early in Grade K, also, children learn to recognize top-to-bottom and left-to-right directions.

ACTIVITY AND OBJECTIVE STATEMENTS

Student pages include **Activity** and **Objective** statements. These provide helpful information to parents and other adults after the pages are used and removed from the book.

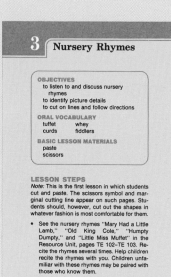

3 Nursery Rhymes

OBJECTIVES
to listen to and discuss nursery rhymes
to identify picture details
to cut on lines and follow directions

ORAL VOCABULARY
tuffet   whey
curds   fiddlers

BASIC LESSON MATERIALS
paste
scissors

LESSON STEPS
Note: This is the first lesson in which students cut and paste. The scissors symbol and marginal cutting line appear on such pages. Students should, however, cut out the shapes in whatever fashion is most comfortable for them.

• See the nursery rhymes "Mary Had a Little Lamb," "Old King Cole," "Humpty Dumpty," and "Little Miss Muffet" in the Resource Unit, pages TE 102–TE 103. Recite the rhymes several times. Help children recite the rhymes with you. Children unfamiliar with these rhymes may be paired with those who know them.

• Explain that pages 4, 5, and 6 go with this lesson. Talk about the pictures and point out spaces for the missing characters.

This lesson is continued on the next two pages.

CUTOUTS

Nursery Rhymes

Child will paste these pictures in sequence on pages 5–6.

4 LITERATURE: Nursery Rhymes   TE 9

TE 10

Lesson 3 (continued)

• On page 4 help children find the character from each rhyme. (Mary, the fiddlers, Humpty Dumpty, Miss Muffet)

• Next ask which character is missing from each picture on pages 5 and 6. Ask the children how they can tell.

• Distribute scissors and paste. Emphasize that scissors and paste must be used carefully. Use blunt scissors and supervise to ensure that paste is not near mouths or eyes.

• Help children to cut out the story characters on page 4. Check their work frequently to see if children need extra help cutting on the lines. Children lacking skill with scissors may need practice cutting straight lines drawn on paper.

• Help children place pictures into the correct spaces on pages 5 and 6. (Humpty Dumpty—page 5 top; Mary—page 5 bottom; Miss Muffet—page 6 top; the fiddlers—page 6 bottom) Before children paste pictures in place, check responses to make sure the children are following directions.

Name

Nursery Rhymes

Child will paste Humpty Dumpty on scene.

Child will paste Mary on scene.

ACTIVITY: listening to nursery rhymes, following directions   OBJECTIVES: to listen to nursery rhymes; to practice cutting and pasting

From Ginn English Program Grade K, copyrighted by Ginn and Company   VISUAL SKILLS: Finding Picture Details 5

HIGH-INTEREST, COLORFUL ART

Lesson pages motivate children through attractive illustrations. Often the colorful art provides visual clues to help children perform the required tasks.

NURSERY RHYMES (continued)

Child will paste Miss Muffet on scene.

Child will paste fiddlers on scene.

6 VISUAL SKILLS: Finding Picture Details

LISTENING/SPEAKING SKILLS

As the group recites a rhyme, have children take turns holding up the page and pointing to the appropriate completed picture.

HELPING ATYPICAL LEARNERS

Disabled: Tape-record the nursery rhymes so that auditory learners may have many individual repetitions. (*Tape Recorder*, A-1) Move from child to child during the cut-and-paste activity. (*Teacher Float*, V-3) Monitor those having trouble with scissors and provide help accordingly. (*Fine-Motor SOS*, D-4)

ADDITIONAL ACTIVITIES

Easy: Have children take turns acting out rhymes as others recite them.

Challenging: Help children recite other familiar rhymes, such as "Old Mother Hubbard" and "Hey, Diddle, Diddle."

TE 11

TEACHER'S EDITION FEATURES

LESSON PLAN

Each instructional lesson plan begins with a list of the lesson **Objective**(s), **Instructional** or **Oral Vocabulary** words, and any **Basic Lesson Materials.**

Specific **Lesson Steps** are provided for introducing the lesson and emphasizing the critical points of instruction.

Easy and **Challenging** activities are provided.

The following features are also provided on a frequent basis:

- opportunities for applying **Listening/Speaking Skills**
- **Extra Information** giving potential errors by students; useful or interesting facts
- **Helping Atypical Learners** with the basic skill lesson; suggestions for the mildly learning disabled, the bilingual Spanish-speaker, and the speaker of nonstandard English

---

15 Telling a Story

OBJECTIVES

to recognize the sequence of events in a story
to identify the main idea of a picture
to retell a story

INSTRUCTIONAL VOCABULARY

top   bottom

ORAL VOCABULARY

cape   connect
hood

BASIC LESSON MATERIALS

crayons—red
paste
scissors

LESSON STEPS

- Have children look at page 23. Point to the pictures from the story "Little Red Riding Hood" on the right side of the page. Distribute paste and blunt scissors. Remind children to use scissors carefully. Help children cut along only the bottom and side dotted lines so that the pictures remain together as a unit. Point out that there are now three rows and that each row has two pictures.

- Ask what is happening in each row of two pictures. Have the children point to each picture as they identify what is happening. Work with only one row at a time.

    row 1—Little Red Riding Hood is leaving her house and waving goodbye to her Mother; next, Little Red Riding Hood is meeting the wolf.
    row 2—Grandmother is running from her house looking very frightened; next, the wolf is in Grandmother's bed talking to Little Red Riding Hood.
    row 3—The wolf is running from Grandmother's house being chased by a wasp; next, Red Riding Hood is eating strawberries and butter with Grandmother and the woodsman.

- Now help children cut out row 1. Remind the children that first, Little Red Riding Hood left her house. Have them find and cut out the picture that shows Red Riding Hood waving goodbye. On page 23, help them find the tree that is numbered 1 and paste the picture on the tree.

- Remind children that next Red Riding Hood met the wolf. Help them find the picture that shows that happening and point to the tree numbered 2 on page 23. Have them paste the picture on the tree.

- Follow a similar procedure with rows 2 and 3, identifying each picture with the children and helping them recognize where to paste each picture. When they have completed the page, review the story asking children what happened first, then next, then next, and so on.

- Although this lesson continues on text page 24, you may wish to break it at this point, completing the remainder in another session.

- Should you wish to complete the lesson in one session, continue with the Lesson Steps on page TE 42.

LISTENING/SPEAKING SKILLS

Help children take turns telling the story "Little Red Riding Hood" using the pictures as aids. Encourage them to use words that indicate the order in which story events happened. (first, next, then, last)

EXTRA INFORMATION

Be aware that some children might have heard other versions of this story and might ask if the grandmother was eaten by the wolf. Explain that this story is very old and that people have told it in many ways. In this story, the grandmother ran away and is safe from the wolf.

Disabled: Before children sequence the pictures, play back the story tape made in Lesson 14 or reread the story. (*Tape Recorder*, A-1) Display the letters A-G for visual learners when they do page 24.

Nonstandard English: Some speakers may use the double negative. ("She don't have no cape.") Model the standard usage for children to hear and repeat.

ADDITIONAL ACTIVITIES

Easy: Have children take turns acting out parts of "Little Red Riding Hood" as you retell the story. Be sure to use words that indicate the order in which the story events happened. *(first, next, then, last)*

Challenging: Have children work in three small groups. Divide a sheet of mural paper into three parts. Choose three main events from the story "Little Red Riding Hood." (Red Riding Hood meets the wolf; the wolf in bed talking to Red Riding Hood; the wolf running from Grandmother's house) Have each group choose one of these three scenes to illustrate. Talk about which picture will be first, next, last. Have groups illustrate the three scenes. Then ask children to retell the story using the finished mural.

This lesson is continued on the next page.

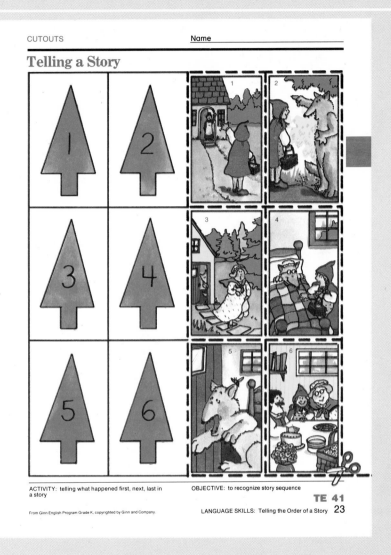

CUTOUTS   Name _____

Telling a Story

ACTIVITY: telling what happened first, next, last in a story

OBJECTIVE: to recognize story sequence

TE 41

From Ginn English Program Grade K, copyrighted by Ginn and Company.

LANGUAGE SKILLS: Telling the Order of a Story   23

EXTRA TEACHER'S EDITION FEATURES

UNIT OPENERS

In Grade K of the **Ginn English Program,** the introduction to each unit includes the following features (see pages TE 3–4 for an example):

■ a list of unit *Objectives*
■ suggestions for *Bulletin Boards* and language *Games*
■ a suggestion to send a *Letter from the Teacher* (blackline reproducible master)
■ suggestions for extensive *Listening Activities*

RESOURCE UNIT

This includes songs, poems, and stories used in conjunction with the lesson plans. (See pages TE 102–109.)

HELPING ATYPICAL LEARNERS

This section describes the **Ginn English Program's** approach to teaching the mildly learning disabled, the bilingual Spanish-speaker, and the speaker of nonstandard English. Charts summarize specific activities that may be used for individual students—and, in many cases, for the entire class—to teach the basic lesson skills. (See pages TE 110–113.)

VOCABULARY TEACHING STRATEGIES

These are suggested activities for developing skills in learning vocabulary. The section includes a complete list of the vocabulary words for Grade K. The list is divided into *Oral Vocabulary* and *Instructional Vocabulary.* (See pages TE 114–115.)

LETTERS FROM THE TEACHER

Three blackline reproducible masters for letters to parents and guardians are provided for your convenience. (See pages TE 116–118.)

SCOPE & SEQUENCE	1	2	3
LANGUAGE	TE page(s)	TE page(s)	TE page(s)
Listening to:			
songs	4, 7–8		83
poems	4	37, 62, 63–64, 72	83
nursery rhymes	9, 10, 11	44	
stories	21–22, 25–26	38, 52, 55, 56, 74, 80	99, 100
Listening for:			
main ideas	9, 11	56	
sequence	25–26	80	
cause and effect		45–46	
details		56, 58–59, 63	84, 87
Speaking			
singing songs	4, 7–8		83, 84, 87
reciting poems, nursery rhymes	4, 9, 11		
speaking to others	5–6		88
telling a story	8, 26	38, 40, 41, 43, 56, 80	99
reciting the alphabet		42	86
talking about:			
feelings	4, 12–15		
nursery rhymes	9–10		
pictures	20, 30	43–44, 74, 76–77, 80	96, 100

SCOPE & SEQUENCE	1	2	3
LANGUAGE (cont'd)	TE page(s)	TE page(s)	TE page(s)
animal homes	24		
animals and their sounds	27	56	
the five senses		37	
cause and effect relationships		45–46	
the weather		70–72	
using complete sentences	7–8, 23, 34	44, 54, 58, 66, 69, 71	92, 96, 98, 100
describing:			
pictures	21, 23, 24	52, 58, 59, 74, 76, 77	92
actions	30		
sensory images		47–48	
directional relationships		67–69	
answering questions		37, 43, 44, 58, 59, 69	
interpreting pictures		45–46, 60, 65–66	
Learning and using words			
direction words (left, right, front, back, up, down, straight ahead, inside, outside, top, bottom, in front of, behind, above, below)	5, 21, 28	65–66, 67–69	
names of people, places, things (nouns)	7, 16, 23	53–54, 65–66	85–86, 87, 89, 96
describing words (adjectives)	12–15, 23–24, 30	47–48, 50–52, 58	

SCOPE & SEQUENCE

LIFE SKILLS	1 TE page(s)	2 TE page(s)	3 TE page(s)
Appreciating the contributions of others	3, 6	56	98–99, 100
Sharing and working together	4, 9, 11, 21, 30	38, 64, 80	86, 88, 90
Introducing oneself	5–6		
Using the senses		37, 47–48, 72	
Identifying parts of the body		47–48	
Classifying objects by function		53–54	
Distinguishing reality and fantasy		62–64	91, 93
Recognizing different environments		65–66, 67–69	93–94
Using a calendar		70–71	
Observing the weather		71–72	
Talking about occupations			82, 98–99, 100
Recognizing the importance of letters and words			82–83, 84–86, 87–88
Talking about safety			96

SCOPE & SEQUENCE

STUDY SKILLS	1 TE page(s)	2 TE page(s)	3 TE page(s)
Using books	3	79–80	99
Using pencils and crayons	6, 16, 24, 30, 32, 34	41–42, 43–44, 46, 48, 51–52, 53–54, 58, 60, 65–66, 71, 74, 76–77, 80	89–90, 92, 95, 96, 97, 100–101
Cutting and pasting	8, 10, 13, 20	38, 40, 51, 56, 60, 68, 77	85, 87
Following oral directions	10, 13, 25–26, 28, 30	40, 47–48, 53–54, 58–59, 65–66, 80	
drawing a circle around	16	43–44, 48, 58, 71, 74, 76–77	88
working in a row	16, 34	40, 43–44, 53–54, 60, 65–66, 74, 76–77	89, 92, 96, 98
marking an X on	34	53–54, 60, 65–66	89, 92, 96, 97
drawing a line from _____ to _____		46	
Recognizing colors	19–20, 23–24, 32	58	82
Recognizing geometric shapes	19–20, 34	52, 74, 80	
Tracing	28, 32		
Classifying objects by size, location, and function		50–52, 53–54, 60, 65–66, 67–68	
Putting letters in alphabetical order			85

SCOPE & SEQUENCE	UNITS		
	1	**2**	**3**
CREATIVE EXPRESSION	TE page(s)	TE page(s)	TE page(s)
Making pictures	3–4, 6, 20, 30	36, 51–52, 60, 71–72, 75	95, 100
Pantomiming and imitating	7, 8, 24	64	83, 99
Dramatizing	11, 15, 27	41, 80	
Dictating stories	15, 21–22		94
Creating oral text for a picture	21		
Imagining		47–48, 50, 60	

SCOPE & SEQUENCE	UNITS		
	1	**2**	**3**
LITERATURE	TE page(s)	TE page(s)	TE page(s)
Nursery rhymes	3, 9	44	
Songs	4, 7–8		83, 84, 87
Poems	4	37, 63–64	83
Stories	8, 21–22, 25–26	38, 40, 43, 44, 52, 55, 56, 80	94–95, 99
Literature Concepts story characters	9, 25–26	38, 52, 55, 56, 58–59, 76–77, 79, 80	
story titles	20, 21	79, 80	
sequence of story events	25–26	40–41	
real and make-believe		62–64	82, 91, 92, 93–94
story events and details		43–44, 50, 52, 58–59	94

Ginn English

Richard L. Venezky
Carol J. Fisher

Ginn and Company

Designers: Gary Fujiwara and Linda Post

Illustrator: Maxie Chambliss

Unit 1

OVERVIEW

Unit 1 emphasizes the communication skills, listening, speaking, interpreting, and following directions. The major instructional goal in this unit is to encourage children to use their language skills effectively to express and receive ideas.

INTRODUCING THE UNIT

Bulletin Boards: Bulletin boards serve as focal points of interest in the classroom and as informal devices for skills development.

- Because Unit 1 focuses attention on the child as an individual *(Lessons 1, 4),* create a display of each child's photo brought from home, or have children draw self-portraits. Title the bulletin board "Here We Are." Gather children around the bulletin board frequently and talk about the photos or drawings. Encourage discussion about the things that make each child unique. Stress the positive contributions of each child in the group.

- On the bulletin board, mount cut outs of the geometric shapes the children will learn about in *Lesson 6.* When cutting out the shape display, use colored construction paper to reinforce the primary colors. Varying the sizes and colors of the shapes will allow children the opportunity to practice the visual matching and discrimination tasks they have been doing. Call the display "All Sorts of Shapes."

- Gather a collection of pictures of baby animals and their parents. Title the display "Animal Families." As the children complete *Lessons 8* and *9,* use the bulletin board to spark discussion and descriptions of animal families and their homes.

- Children today are often unfamiliar with traditional nursery rhymes and tales. *Lesson 3* acquaints children with some of these favorites. A bulletin board entitled "Nursery Rhyme Friends" could provide a stimulus for retelling, further discussion, and attention to the details of the rhymes. Display pictures of nursery rhyme characters. Use the display to encourage children to add more nursery rhymes. Have them look in books or ask persons at home to help them learn about additional nursery rhyme "friends."

Game: To enhance visual discrimination and visual memory, play a game called "Naughty Squirrel." Place four classroom items on a table. Have the children walk around the table. Tell them to look at the items and try to remember them. Have children take turns being "it" and the "Naughty Squirrel." Have the child who is "it" close his or her eyes. "Naughty Squirrel" takes one item away. The child who is "it" then opens his or her eyes and tries to remember what the "Naughty Squirrel" took away. Increase or decrease the number of classroom items according to the needs and abilities of the children.

Letter from the Teacher: You may wish to distribute copies of *Letter 1 from the Teacher* (page TE 116) for children to take home at this time.

Unit 1 (continued)

LISTENING/SPEAKING ACTIVITIES

The following activities for developing listening and speaking skills may accompany any lesson within the unit and may be done at any time during the unit. (*Note:* If activities are spread over several days or weeks, the selection or song should be reviewed each time.)

ACTIVITY 1

Objectives

to practice listening
to respond by singing a single refrain

Procedure

Teach the echo song "Morning Greeting," Resource Unit, TE 102. Children will echo the teacher's "Good morning." Sing the song several times encouraging children to join you.

The song may be used daily during the unit to bring children into the group, to encourage interaction with others, and to give children practice responding correctly and at appropriate times.

ACTIVITY 2

Objectives

to practice listening to a poem
to use appropriate words to discuss feelings
to share similar experiences

Procedure

Have students listen to the poem "Tiptoe," Resource Unit, TE 102, as an activity for "quiet time." Talk about doing special tricks just for fun, such as keeping off the cracks in the sidewalk. Tell the children that this poem tells the story of a child who decides to tiptoe all day.

After reading the poem, ask children to recall experiences they have had doing something "just for fun" and how children felt while doing them. Reread the poem and encourage children to join you as they become familiar with it. Finally, have children draw pictures to illustrate how they think the child in the poem looked while tiptoeing.

1 Telling Who I Am

LESSON STEPS

Note: The instructional vocabulary listed above
may require specific preteaching. The first two
Lesson Steps suggest a way to do this.

- Help children understand what it means to
  introduce yourself to a friend. Say: "This
  means we tell our names to each other in a
  clear voice. It's also nice to say 'Hello.' I'll
  show you what I mean." Model for the
  group several times saying: "Hello, my
  name is _____."

- Ask the group to say "Hello" to you. Show
  children what you mean by *left, right, front,
  back.* Then ask children to introduce themselves to those to the left, right, front, and
  back of them. Have them say: "Hello, my
  name is _____."

This lesson is continued on the next page.

Name _____

Telling Who I Am

Child will draw picture of
himself or herself here.

ME

ACTIVITY: drawing a self-portrait   OBJECTIVE: to introduce oneself to the group

LIFE AND STUDY SKILLS: Telling Who I Am   1

Lesson 1 (continued)

- Then help children turn to page 1. Point out the picture frame and the empty space. Tell children that the frame needs a picture.

- Hold up the page and point to the word *me*. Ask children what the word *me* means to them. Encourage them to point to themselves and say their names. Tell the group: "Pictures of *you* are special because each of you is special—there's only one *you*." To clarify, point to yourself, say your name, and add the fact that you are a special *me*, too—the only one with your name, your hair, eyes, and so on.

- Distribute crayons and have children draw pictures of themselves inside the frames.

- When children have completed their self-portraits, encourage them to hold up their drawings, one at a time, and say: "This is me."

HELPING ATYPICAL LEARNERS

Disabled: Move about the room as children draw. Make note of those having difficulty. (*Teacher Float,* V-3) They may copy or trace a model made by you. (*Model T,* V-1)

ADDITIONAL ACTIVITIES

Easy: Encourage children to listen carefully when others are speaking. Add that: "When you talk, remember to look at the person you are talking to, rather than the floor or ceiling." Remind children to speak clearly so that everyone can hear.

Then have two or three children tell their names. Have others listen to remember and then repeat the names in order. Let children take turns playing each role—naming themselves, repeating the names of others in the class. Praise their efforts.

Challenging: Print name tags for children. Then, on separate paper, make dashed outlines of the letters of their names for tracing, using the tags as models. Encourage children to copy their names at least two or three times.

Telling What I See

Telling What I See

ACTIVITY: listening to and singing a song   OBJECTIVE: to learn a song

OBJECTIVES

to respond in complete sentences
to listen to and sing a song
to pantomime and imitate actions

ORAL VOCABULARY

winding   sparrow
bank   church steeple

BASIC LESSON MATERIALS

LESSON STEPS

- See the song "A Little Boy Went Walking," in the Resource Unit, page TE 103.

- Talk with the children about the pictures on pages 2 and 3 of their books. Tell them that the pictures show a boy walking. Ask what the boy sees. (rabbit, river with fish, birds, bridge, and church with steeple) Encourage children to respond in complete sentences. Explain any pictures that may be unfamiliar.

- Tell children that there is a song to go with the pictures. Have them listen as you sing the song, making appropriate hand/arm motions for the hopping rabbit, winding river, flying birds, the boy resting his head on his arms at the bridge, the steeple shape, and the boy going to tell his mother what he has seen. Encourage children to follow the picture as you sing the song.

This lesson is continued on the next page.

Lesson 2 (continued)

- Sing the song again. Encourage children to sing and move with you as they become familiar with the song.

LISTENING/SPEAKING SKILLS

Talk about how a song can tell a story. Ask children to tell the "story" this song tells. Encourage them to use complete sentences.

HELPING ATYPICAL LEARNERS

Disabled: Play *Simon Says* (*Play-Off,* D-2) to practice the movements in the song. Tape-record the song so that auditory learners may have many individual repetitions. (*Tape Recorder,* A-1)

Nonstandard English: If possible, tape-record the song "A Little Boy Went Walking" so that children hear and become familiar with standard pronunciation.

ADDITIONAL ACTIVITIES

Easy: On oak tag draw simple pictures of a boy, rabbit, river, fish, nest, bird, cloud, and church steeple. Children might help you cut them out. Have children take turns moving the manipulatives as the song "A Little Boy Went Walking" is sung.

Challenging: Suggest that children might want to sing "A Little Boy Went Walking" at home for their families. Or you might have them sing it for another class.

3 Nursery Rhymes

LESSON STEPS

Note: This is the first lesson in which students cut and paste. The scissors symbol and marginal cutting line appear on such pages. Students should, however, cut out the shapes in whatever fashion is most comfortable for them.

- See the nursery rhymes "Mary Had a Little Lamb," "Old King Cole," "Humpty Dumpty," and "Little Miss Muffet" in the Resource Unit, pages TE 102–TE 103. Recite the rhymes several times. Help children recite the rhymes with you. Children unfamiliar with these rhymes may be paired with those who know them.

- Explain that pages 4, 5, and 6 go with this lesson. Talk about the pictures and point out spaces for the missing characters.

This lesson is continued on the next two pages.

Nursery Rhymes

Child will paste these pictures in sequence on pages 5–6.

Lesson 3 (continued)

- On page 4 help children find the character from each rhyme. (Mary, the fiddlers, Humpty Dumpty, Miss Muffet)

- Next ask which character is missing from each picture on pages 5 and 6. Ask the children how they can tell.

- Distribute scissors and paste. Emphasize that scissors and paste must be used carefully. Use blunt scissors and supervise to ensure that paste is not near mouths or eyes.

- Help children to cut out the story characters on page 4. Check their work frequently to see if children need extra help cutting on the lines. Children lacking skill with scissors may need practice cutting straight lines drawn on paper.

- Help children place pictures into the correct spaces on pages 5 and 6. (Humpty Dumpty—page 5 top; Mary—page 5 bottom; Miss Muffet—page 6 top; the fiddlers—page 6 bottom) Before children paste pictures in place, check responses to make sure the children are following directions.

Nursery Rhymes

Child will paste Humpty Dumpty on scene.

Child will paste Mary on scene.

ACTIVITY: listening to nursery rhymes, following directions

OBJECTIVES: to listen to nursery rhymes; to practice cutting and pasting

VISUAL SKILLS: Finding Picture Details 5

Child will paste Miss Muffet on scene.

Child will paste fiddlers on scene.

LISTENING/SPEAKING SKILLS

As the group recites a rhyme, have children take turns holding up the page and pointing to the appropriate completed picture.

HELPING ATYPICAL LEARNERS

Disabled: Tape-record the nursery rhymes so that auditory learners may have many individual repetitions. (*Tape Recorder,* A-1) Move from child to child during the cut-and-paste activity. (*Teacher Float,* V-3) Monitor those having trouble with scissors and provide help accordingly. (*Fine-Motor SOS,* D-4)

ADDITIONAL ACTIVITIES

Easy: Have children take turns acting out rhymes as others recite them.

Challenging: Help children recite other familiar rhymes, such as "Old Mother Hubbard" and "Hey, Diddle, Diddle."

Telling How I Feel

LESSON STEPS

- Have children look at page 7 and tell how they think the person in the picture feels. (happy) Ask: "How can you tell?" (corners of mouth up, eyes open, eyebrows raised) Talk about what might make a person happy.

- Have children look at page 8 and tell how they think the person in the picture feels and how they can tell. (sad; corners of mouth turned down, bottom lip out, eyes downcast) Talk about what might make a person sad.

Name

Telling How I Feel

ACTIVITY: talking about how we feel   OBJECTIVE: to identify feelings and emotions

LANGUAGE SKILLS: Talking about Feelings

Telling How I Feel

- Follow the same procedure for the pictures on pages 9 and 10. (page 9: angry—tightly closed mouth, eyes made small, brows pulled together; page 10: surprised—open mouth, wide eyes, raised eyebrows) Talk about what might make a person angry or surprised.

- Distribute blunt scissors. Emphasize that scissors must be used carefully. Tell children that if they cut out the pictures on pages 7 and 9 very carefully they will have a surprise. (Turned over, each picture reveals a different face.)

- After children have cut out the pictures, help them see that the faces on each side show different feelings.

- Help children tape neck tabs to wooden stirrers or tongue depressors and see how turning the hand masks reveals faces with different feelings on each side.

- Read the following sentences aloud. Ask children to hold up the hand mask that they think shows how the person described in each feels. Expect different responses.

  Carla just learned to ride a two-wheeler.
  Bob's team just lost the big game.
  When Ray opened the door, everyone shouted "Surprise!"
  Philip's favorite toy was broken by someone.

This lesson is continued on the next two pages.

TE 13

Lesson 3 (continued)

LISTENING/SPEAKING SKILLS

Ask children to think of a time they might feel happy or surprised. Ask if they wish to share it as they show the hand mask that shows how they would feel.

HELPING ATYPICAL LEARNERS

Disabled: Students may require help from you or each other in cutting out the faces. (*Fine-Motor SOS,* D-4)

Nonstandard English: Some speakers use the verb *be* to indicate action that is ongoing. Watch for the verb form "I be sad" or "I be happy." Model sentences using *am* for students to repeat.

TE 14

Telling How I Feel

LANGUAGE SKILLS: Talking about Feelings   **9**

Telling How I Feel

ADDITIONAL ACTIVITIES

Easy: Encourage children to try changing their facial expressions to represent the words *happy, sad, angry,* and *surprised.*

Challenging: Have children choose one or more of the four feelings they have talked about (happy, sad, angry, surprised) and dictate a chart story about someone who feels those emotions. They might use their hand masks to retell the story.

5 Alike and Different

LESSON STEPS

Note: The instructional vocabulary listed, may require specific preteaching. Suggestions are included here as part of the Lesson Steps.

• Draw a star on the chalkboard. Demonstrate how to draw a circle around the star. Have children draw circles in the air.

• Display two classroom items that are alike. (two pencils, books, crayons) Ask children to talk about them. (They are alike.)

• Help them find row 1 on page 11 by finding the boy from the song "A Little Boy Went Walking." This is row 1. If children are having difficulty following rows, they may need to use row liners made of 2″ wide strips of oak tag. Name the pictures with the children. (bird, flower, bird) Have children find two pictures that are alike and circle them. (birds)

• Tell children that row 2 begins with a picture of a rabbit. Help them name the pictures and circle the two pictures that are alike. (fish)

• Have children find row 3, which begins with the picture of a nest. Have them find and circle the two pictures that are alike. (flowers)

HELPING ATYPICAL LEARNERS

Disabled: Precede the lesson with *Simon Says* (*Play-Off,* D-2), emphasizing the Instructional Vocabulary words. When questioning children about items that are alike and different, focus their thinking by asking Yes-No questions. (*Yes-No Questions,* D-1)

ADDITIONAL ACTIVITIES

Easy: Assemble a random display of pairs of classroom items. (books, chalk, erasers, blocks, picture cards, letters) Have children put together the items that are alike.

Challenging: Assemble a random display of pairs of classroom items. (books, pencils, chalk, caryons, shapes) Have children put together items that are alike. Encourage them to use words that describe the items and to tell why they are alike. (*smooth, yellow, wooden, square, rough, large*)

Alike and Different

1.

2.

3.

ACTIVITY: circling two pictures that are alike   OBJECTIVE: to recognize pictures that are alike

LIFE AND STUDY SKILLS: Following Directions 11

6 Shapes and Colors

OBJECTIVES

to identify geometric shapes: circle, square, rectangle, triangle

to identify colors: green, yellow, orange, red

to follow directions

INSTRUCTIONAL VOCABULARY

rectangle   triangle

square

BASIC LESSON MATERIALS

classroom items (blocks, shape and color cards, box tops, crayons)

paste

scissors

Shapes and Colors

Shapes and Colors

Child will paste shapes from page 12 to form a picture here.

ACTIVITY: creating a design using the four basic shapes   OBJECTIVE: to recognize the four basic shapes

LESSON STEPS

- Display a group of classroom items that are circles, rectangles, triangles, and squares. Help children name the shapes. Then ask them to look around the classroom and find other items that are circles (toy wheel, clock face), squares (box top, table), rectangles (door, desk), and triangles (musical instrument, building block).

- Display a group of classroom items that includes the colors green, yellow, blue, and red. (crayons, color cards, paint jars) Help children name the colors. Then ask them to look around the classroom and find other items that are green, yellow, blue, and red.

- Have children look at the shapes on page 12. Display a square from the group of classroom items. Say: "This is a square. Find a square on your paper and put your finger on it." Check responses. Talk about what squares look like. (four sides that are the same size, and four corners) Point to the sides and corners as you talk about them. Ask children the colors of the squares on the page.

- Display a rectangle and name it. Have children point to the rectangles on the page and repeat the word *rectangle.* Talk about what rectangles look like. (two long sides that are the same size, two short sides that are the same size, four corners) Point to the sides and corners as you talk about them. Ask children to name the colors of the rectangles on the page.

This lesson is continued on the next page.

Lesson 6 (continued)

- Display a circle and name it. Have children find the circles on the page. Talk about what circles look like. Emphasize a circle's roundness by drawing circles in the air. Ask children to name the colors of the circles on the page.

- Display a triangle and name it. Have children find the triangles on the page. Talk about what triangles look like. (three sides, three corners) Point to the sides and corners as you talk about them. Ask children to name the colors of the triangles on the page.

- Distribute paste and scissors. Have children cut out the shapes on page 12. Ask them to place the shapes any way they like within the frame on page 13 to make a picture. Encourage children to move the shapes around until they have formed a picture they like. Then have them paste the shapes in place. Ask them to think of a name for their pictures. Write the titles on the name plates for them.

LISTENING/SPEAKING SKILLS

Encourage children to take turns telling about their pictures. Have them hold up their designs and share the names they decided to use.

HELPING ATYPICAL LEARNERS

Disabled: Tell children that a square looks the same no matter which side is on the bottom. Demonstrate this concept by holding up a square different ways and asking if it looks the same or different. Do the same for a rectangle and compare the answers.

Spanish Speaking: To help build vocabulary, have each student name at least three common nouns that name classroom objects. (example: *desk, scissors, clock*)

ADDITIONAL ACTIVITIES

Easy: Hold up one shape at a time from the group of classroom items and ask children to identify the shape.

Challenging: Ask children to think of things that are shaped like a circle. (balloon, the moon, ball, a car tire)

7 Telling a Story

LESSON STEPS

- Have children look at page 14 and talk about what is happening in the picture. (a circus) Ask what is happening inside each circus ring. (A trainer is working with a lion and a tiger; a clown and a pig are doing their acts near a man balanced on a ladder; bears are balancing on large balls.) Ask what animal is outside the rings. (elephant)

- Help children dictate a story about the picture. Encourage them to use the oral vocabulary in the lesson. Write the story on the chalkboard or on chart paper. Help children select a title for their story. Read the story aloud.

- You might ask children who are able whether they can find a sentence or a word that they can read by themselves.

This lesson is continued on the next page.

Telling a Story

ACTIVITY: telling a story about a picture

OBJECTIVE: to recognize picture details; to tell a story about a picture

HELPING ATYPICAL LEARNERS

Disabled: Begin sentences for students having difficulty in telling the picture story in words. Provide the noun phrase. Have students supply the verb phrase.

ADDITIONAL ACTIVITIES

Easy: Encourage children to dictate an experience story about a familiar subject, such as school. You might begin with a sentence such as "We go to school." Reading experience stories aloud helps reinforce the concept that what we say can be written.

Challenging: Talk about the jobs of people who work in a circus. (acrobat, clown, ringmaster, lion tamer, juggler) Ask children to choose the job they would most like to have. Then have them draw a picture of themselves working in the circus doing the job they chose.

8 | Talking about Animals

LESSON STEPS

- Have children look at the pictures on page 15 and name the animals. (squirrels, birds, rabbits) Encourage children to describe the animals using complete sentences. ("I see a gray squirrel.") Remind them to use the oral vocabulary they have been learning.

This lesson is continued on the next page.

Talking about Animals

ACTIVITY: matching pictures of baby animals and adult animals

OBJECTIVE: to compare baby animals and adult animals

Lesson 8 (continued)

- Explain that some of the pictures show baby animals and others show grown-up animals. Point out the rectangle below each picture. Ask children to point to the picture of the grown-up squirrel. Then have them find the baby squirrels. Tell children to choose one color crayon and to color the insides of the rectangles below both pictures the same color. Repeat this procedure with the birds and the rabbits, choosing a different color for each pair.

- After the animals are matched, talk about how these animals are alike. (They are little, each has a tail.) Ask: "How is a squirrel different from a rabbit?" (A squirrel has a bigger tail and smaller ears.) "How is a bird different from a rabbit?" (Birds fly, rabbits hop.) Encourage the use of as many descriptive words as possible. You might ask children to describe how they think each animal might feel to touch. (soft, furry, smooth, feathery, warm)

HELPING ATYPICAL LEARNERS
Disabled: Ask *Yes-No Questions* (D-1) about the animals to focus on specific characteristics of the animals; for example: "Are the ears of a rabbit the same as the ears of a squirrel?" (*Model T,* V-1)

ADDITIONAL ACTIVITIES
Easy: Talk about animal homes. Ask children if they have seen where any animals live. (in a tree, underground, near the water) Children might like to pantomime the actions of an animal and have others guess the animal's identity.

Challenging: Talk about the differences between pet animals and wild animals. Make an *Animal* booklet by finding pictures of animals in magazines and cutting out the pictures. Paste pictures of pet animals in one part of the booklet and wild animals in another.

9 Listening to a Story

LESSON STEPS

- See the story "Little Duckling Tries His Voice," Resource Unit, page TE 104.

- Tell the children they will hear a story about a little duckling who tries to make different sounds. Ask them to listen carefully to see what happens.

- Ask children to follow the pictures as you read the story. You might direct them to point to the picture of the duckling and the cat as you read that part of the story.

This lesson is continued on the next two pages.

Listening to a Story

Child will paste these pictures in sequence on page 17.

Lesson 9 (continued)

- As you read, encourage children to make the sounds each animal in the story makes. Have children point to the pictures as they make the sounds.

- When you have finished reading, ask: "Who did Little Duckling meet first?" (the cat) Then ask them to point to the picture that shows what happened first. (the cat and duckling on the barnyard road) Ask: "Who did Little Duckling meet next?" (the dog) "Which picture shows that happening?" (the duckling and the dog) Reread parts of the story if needed. Continue until children have identified all the story happenings in order and have found the appropriate pictures in order.

- Talk about the fact that the pictures tell the story by telling what happened first, next, last.

- Distribute paste and scissors. Help children cut out the pictures on page 16. Point out the numbers 1, 2, 3, 4, and 5. As you talk about the order in which story events happened, have the children position the cutout pictures on page 17. Check responses before children paste the pictures.

LISTENING/SPEAKING SKILL

When they have completed page 17, some children might wish to retell the story in their own words using the pictures to help them tell story events in order. Have others listen as the story is retold.

TE 26

Listening to a Story

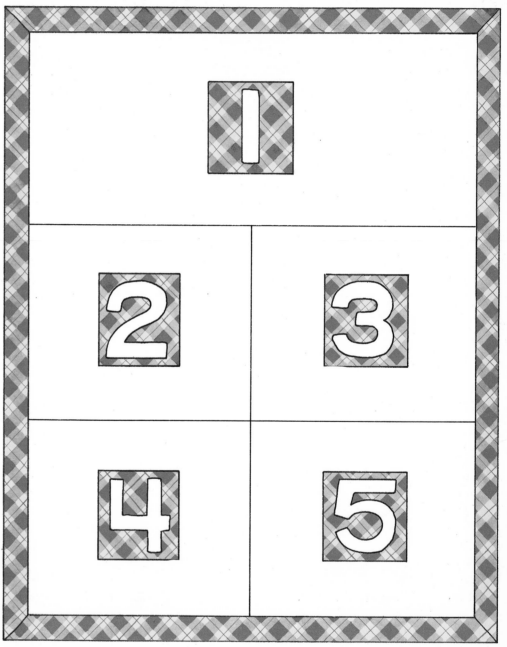

ACTIVITY: placing story pictures in correct order   OBJECTIVE: to recognize a sequence of story events

HELPING ATYPICAL LEARNERS

Disabled: Tape-record the story as you read it to the class. (*Tape Recorder,* A-1) After discussing the pictures, play the story as students arrange the pictures in order. Play *Simon Says* with animal sounds. (*Play-Off,* D-2)

Nonstandard English: Speakers of nonstandard English may not pronounce the *-ed* at the end of past tense regular verbs. ("He walk.") Watch for this usage and model standard usage for children to hear and practice.

ADDITIONAL ACTIVITIES

Easy: Prepare oak tag cutouts of a cat, dog, bird, cow, and duck, or ask children to draw the animals. Place the pictures in order in the chalk tray or on a feltboard. Explain that the pictures show which animals the duckling met first, then next, then next, and so on. (cat, dog, bird, cow, duck) Have children take turns holding up each animal and retelling the part of the story that includes the pictured animal. Before each child tells his or her part of the story, say: "First, Little Duckling met the cat." ("Next, he met the dog," etc.)

Challenging: Talk about other animals that are often found in a barnyard. (horse, goat, sheep, pig) Ask what might have happened if Little Duckling had met one of these animals. Encourage children to act out these scenes using the sounds each animal makes. (horse—neigh; goat—naa; sheep—baa; pig—oink)

OBJECTIVES
to follow oral directions
to trace a path through a maze
to practice small motor skills

INSTRUCTIONAL VOCABULARY
up   down

ORAL VOCABULARY
trapped

BASIC LESSON MATERIALS
crayons

LESSON STEPS

• Have children look at the picture on page 18 and talk about what is happening. (A fish is trapped in a net.)

• Tell children they can help the fish escape. Have them put their fingers on the fish as a starting point. Help them move their fingers through the broken parts of the net until they get all the way through the net.

• As children trace the way through the net with their fingers, give oral directions such as "Go right. Stop. Go up. Stop. Go left. Stop."

• After children have done this several times, have them trace the fish's path with a pencil or crayon.

HELPING ATYPICAL LEARNERS
Disabled: Use the Instructional Vocabulary in a game of *Simon Says.* For example, tell students, "Simon says move your right hand up." (*Play-Off,* D-2) Work on mazes with dependent learners. (*Teacher-Student Dialogue,* A-2b) Visual and auditory learners work in pairs to do the maze. (*Student-Pair Dialogue,* A-2a)

ADDITIONAL ACTIVITIES
Easy: Trace a simple maze on the chalkboard or on chart paper. Have children pretend to be the fish, following oral directions for escape. Use direction words such as "Go left. Now go up. Go right."

Challenging: Have children draw a fish and decorate it to their liking. Encourage them to make up a story about their fish. As a story starter, suggest a title, or ask pupils to do so, such as "Brave Little Fish," "How My Fish Escaped," and so on.

Tracing a Path

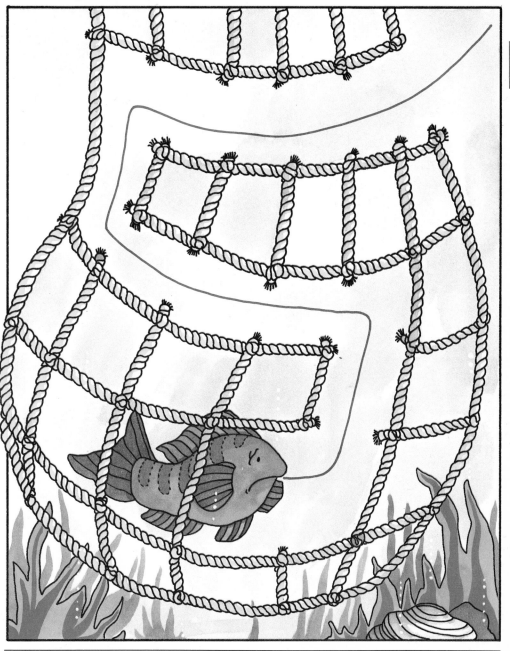

ACTIVITY: finding a path out of a maze   OBJECTIVE: to follow directions

What Will Happen?

OBJECTIVES
to describe actions and predict outcomes

to observe, interpret, and generalize about picture details

to follow directions

ORAL VOCABULARY
creeping

BASIC LESSON MATERIALS
crayons

LESSON STEPS

- Have children look at and talk about each picture on page 19. Ask: "What animal do you think this story is about? Where is the kitten? What is the kitten doing? What does the kitten see? Is the mouse real? How do you know? What do you think will happen next?" Allow time for discussion.

- Encourage children to use words such as *peeking, creeping,* and *looking* as they describe the kitten's actions. Then ask what they think will happen to the mouse. Ask: "Will the kitten be fooled? How do you know?"

- Encourage children to talk about what they think will happen next. In the space provided, have them illustrate what they think the kitten will do next. Ask: "How do you think the story will end?" When the children have finished, ask several of them to explain their drawings. Talk about how these story endings are alike or different.

ADDITIONAL ACTIVITIES

Easy: Have children draw an animal they would like to have as a pet. Then draw three things this pet can do. Ask them to share and explain their pictures.

Challenging: Ask three children each to tell part of the story of the cat and the toy mouse in order. Have them begin with the words *first, next,* and *last,* as appropriate. Encourage them to use the pictures as clues. Have children make up a title for the story. ("The Kitten and the Mouse," "The Kitten's Surprise," and so on)

What Will Happen?

Child will illustrate
possible story ending.

ACTIVITY: drawing a picture that shows what
happens at the end of a story

OBJECTIVE: to predict the outcome of a story

TE 31

LANGUAGE SKILLS: Telling What Will Happen **19**

OBJECTIVES

to use a crayon or pencil to trace

to follow directions, oral and printed

to recognize colors green, blue,
    red, brown

BASIC LESSON MATERIALS

crayons—green, blue, red, brown

LESSON STEPS

- Use arrows to form the outline of a large circle on the chalkboard. Place a starting dot at the top of the circle. Demonstrate how to complete the outline by following the arrows.

- If you have colored chalk, repeat the activity above in another color.

- Have children look at the picture on page 20. Ask what animal is hiding in the picture. (cat) Point to the cat's head, tail, body, and legs. Tell the children that they can finish the picture by following the arrows. The arrows tell which way to move the crayon and what color crayon to use.

- Say: "Start with your green crayon. Find the starting dot on the cat's head. Move your green crayon along the green arrows the way the arrows point."

- Say: "Find the cat's body. Use your blue crayon and start on the blue starting dot. Now find the cat's tail and the red starting dot. Use your red crayon to finish the tail. Finish the cat's legs with a brown crayon." Remind children to use the starting dots and follow the direction of the arrows.

- Check responses frequently to make sure that children are following directions correctly.

HELPING ATYPICAL LEARNERS

Spanish Speaking: Have each student give at least three proper nouns that could name a cat or dog.

ADDITIONAL ACTIVITIES

Easy: Draw simple, large shapes on the chalkboard (circles, triangles, and squares) using arrows for outlines. Have children practice following the arrows with chalk to complete the shapes.

Challenging: Have children think of a name for the cat they finished on page 20. Ask what a cat feels like to touch. Encourage children to use complete sentences and to use words such as *furry, soft, fuzzy,* and *warm.*

Following Directions

ACTIVITY: completing a picture   OBJECTIVE: to understand how to follow directions

Alike and Different

LESSON STEPS

- On the chalkboard demonstrate how to make the letter *X*. Have children make an *X* in the air several times.

- Have children look at page 21 and find the duckling at the beginning of row 1.

- Help children name the shapes in the row. (circle, circle, square) Ask them which shapes are the same. (circles) Which shape does not belong? (square) Have them mark an *X* on the shape that does not belong in the row. (square)

- Have children find the dog at the beginning of row 2. Help them name the shapes. (triangle, circle, triangle) Say: "Mark an *X* on the shape that does not belong in this row." (circle)

- Follow a similar procedure for rows 3 and 4, having children mark *X* on the shapes that do not belong in the rows. (row 3—triangle; row 4—rectangle)

HELPING ATYPICAL LEARNERS

Disabled: On separate pieces of paper, draw or have pairs of children draw two rectangles, two squares, two circles, and two triangles. One partner arranges a group of two like shapes and one different shape. The other tells which shapes are the same and which shape is different. (*Student-Pair Dialogue,* A-2a)

ADDITIONAL ACTIVITIES

Easy: Draw several groups of shapes on the chalkboard, two shapes the same and one different. Have children take turns identifying the shape that does not belong in the group. Encourage them to use complete sentences when identifying the shape. ("I see two circles and only one square.")

Challenging: Display several groups of classroom items, two items the same, one different. (two pieces of chalk, one pencil; two books that are the same, one different; two rectangular blocks, one square) Have children identify the item that does not belong in each group. Then ask: "Why doesn't it belong?" Encourage children to answer in complete sentences.

Alike and Different

1.  ○ ○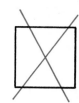

2.   △   △

3.   ☐ ☐

4.  ☐ ☐

ACTIVITY: marking an X on the picture that is different   OBJECTIVE: to recognize pictures that are alike and different

LIFE AND STUDY SKILLS: Following Directions

Unit 2

OVERVIEW

Instructional tasks in Unit 2 increase in complexity, expanding the skills developed in Unit 1. Children use their communication skills by asking and answering questions, listening to and creating stories, identifying and talking about the five senses, and recognizing and recalling the events in a story.

INTRODUCING THE UNIT
Bulletin Boards

- Since much attention in Unit 2 is focused on learning about and examining the world around us—the touch, sound, sight, smell, and taste of things—prepare a bulletin board titled "What in the World Is This?" Mount several interesting pictures of unusual objects or of activities that are not immediately obvious. Examples include: water spouting from the sea (a whale is underwater); crowd cheering in the stands (watching a ball game); a rainbow (after it has rained).

  Encourage children to use picture clues to guess what is happening in the picture. Emphasize that many different possibilities exist and encourage a variety of responses. Accept all reasonable guesses.

- The children will be learning to sequence events in a story during this unit. A bulletin board called "Jolly Jumbles" can reinforce the skill. Depending on the ability and needs of individual children, this display could feature letters of the alphabet or numerals in random order, children's drawings of things they usually do in the morning, afternoon, and at night (getting dressed, going to or from school, sleeping), or frames from individual cartoons cut apart and mounted.

  Have children talk about the order in which things happen, using the instructional vocabulary they have been learning. (first, next, then, last) Before the display is taken down, have children put the objects or pictures in proper sequence.

Game: Encourage children to use their sense of touch to learn about the world. Put common classroom items in a drawstring bag or box into which you have cut a hole large enough for a child's hand and arm. You might place a marble, a rubber ball, a crayon, a coin, an eraser in the bag. Choose children to identify the objects entirely by touch. Make the objects more difficult to identify as children become accustomed to the game.

Letter from the Teacher: You may wish to distribute copies of *Letter 2 from the Teacher* (page TE 117) for children to take home at this time.

LISTENING/SPEAKING ACTIVITIES

The following activities for developing listening and speaking skills may accompany any lesson within the unit and may be done at any time during the unit. (*Note:* If the activity is spread over several days or weeks, the selection or song should be reviewed each time.)

ACTIVITY 1

Objectives
to discuss the five senses

Procedure
Explain that we learn about our world by seeing, hearing, touching, smelling, and tasting. Encourage children to use words that describe sensory images in this manner:

See—ask children to look out the window and talk about something they see.

Hear—clap your hands, snap your fingers, or whistle. Ask children to talk about what they heard.

Touch—have available pieces of fabric, wood, metal, paper, or feathers for children and ask how the materials feel.

Smell—give examples such as flowers, fresh-baked bread, onions, wood burning. Ask children to talk about how these things smell.

Taste—talk about the taste of different kinds of food. (apple, carrot, hamburger, banana, milk, pickles) Do this activity several times. Children will add new sensory experiences as they talk about things they learn through the senses.

ACTIVITY 2

Objectives
to listen to a poem
to answer questions accurately

Procedure
Explain that asking many questions and wanting to know why and how things happen is called *curiosity*. Read the poem "Curiosity" by Harry Behn, Resource Unit, page TE 104. Talk about the poem. Reread some of the questions the poet asks. Ask if children can answer any of the questions. Discuss questions children might want to add to the poem.

Ask children if there are things they wonder about. Tell them that school is a place where curious people find out how and why things happen. Stress that books give us much of the information we want.

OBJECTIVES
to listen to a story
to create dialogue
to perform a finger play

ORAL VOCABULARY

wood	mill
stung	dash
hoarse	underbrush
wasp	bouquet
velvet	cottage

BASIC LESSON MATERIALS
scissors
tape

LESSON STEPS

- See the story "Little Red Riding Hood," Resource Unit, page TE 105–TE 106. Tell the children they will hear a story about a little girl who went through the woods to take her grandmother a present. Ask them to listen and find out what happens.

- Read the story "Little Red Riding Hood" aloud.

- After reading the story, have children look at the story characters on page 22. Identify the pictures with the children. (Little Red Riding Hood, the wolf, Grandmother, the wasp, the woodsman) Explain that the pictures can be cut out and made into finger puppets.

- Distribute blunt scissors. Remind the children to use scissors carefully. Supervise as they cut out the puppets. Distribute tape and help children tape the tabs together. Show them how to fit the puppets on their fingers. Read the story again, showing children how and when to move their finger puppets.

- Have children practice telling parts of the story using the finger puppets as actors.

HELPING ATYPICAL LEARNERS

Disabled: Tape-record "Little Red Riding Hood" as you read the story. Play back the tape, first as students cut out puppets and then as they act out the story. (*Tape Recorder,* A-1) Assist students having trouble with scissors. (*Fine-Motor SOS,* D-4)

Spanish Speaking: To help build vocabulary, pick an object and have students list all the words they can think of that describe how the object looks. For further practice, choose a new object.

ADDITIONAL ACTIVITIES

Easy: Have children work in pairs and use their finger puppets to act out the story for each other.

Challenging: Ask children to use words to describe each of the finger puppet characters. List the words they suggest. You might suggest such words as *brave, strong* (woodsman); *helpful, friendly, brave* (Little Red Riding Hood); *sly, smart* (wolf); *kind, frightened* (Grandmother).

Listening to a Story

ACTIVITY: listening to and retelling a story using finger puppets

OBJECTIVE: to retell a story

OBJECTIVES
to recognize the sequence of events in a story
to identify the main idea of a picture
to retell a story

INSTRUCTIONAL VOCABULARY
top   bottom

ORAL VOCABULARY
cape   connect
hood

BASIC LESSON MATERIALS
crayons—red
paste
scissors

LESSON STEPS

- Have children look at page 23. Point to the pictures from the story "Little Red Riding Hood" on the right side of the page. Distribute paste and blunt scissors. Remind children to use scissors carefully. Help children cut along only the bottom and side dotted lines so that the pictures remain together as a unit. Point out that there are now three rows and that each row has two pictures.

- Ask what is happening in each row of two pictures. Have the children point to each picture as they identify what is happening. Work with only one row at a time.

  row 1—Little Red Riding Hood is leaving her house and waving goodbye to her Mother; next, Little Red Riding Hood is meeting the wolf.
  row 2—Grandmother is running from her house looking very frightened; next, the wolf is in Grandmother's bed talking to Little Red Riding Hood.
  row 3—The wolf is running from Grandmother's house being chased by a wasp; next, Red Riding Hood is eating strawberries and butter with Grandmother and the woodsman.

- Now help children cut out row 1. Remind the children that first, Little Red Riding Hood left her house. Have them find and cut out the picture that shows Red Riding Hood waving goodbye. On page 23, help them find the tree that is numbered 1 and paste the picture on the tree.

- Remind children that next Red Riding Hood met the wolf. Help them find the picture that shows that happening and point to the tree numbered 2 on page 23. Have them paste the picture on the tree.

- Follow a similar procedure with rows 2 and 3, identifying each picture with the children and helping them recognize where to paste each picture. When they have completed the page, review the story asking children what happened first, then next, then next, and so on.

- Although this lesson continues on text page 24, you may wish to break it at this point, completing the remainder in another session.

- Should you wish to complete the lesson in one session, continue with the Lesson Steps on page TE 42.

LISTENING/SPEAKING SKILLS

Help children take turns telling the story "Little Red Riding Hood" using the pictures as aids. Encourage them to use words that indicate the order in which story events happened. *(first, next, then, last)*

EXTRA INFORMATION

Be aware that some children might have heard other versions of this story and might ask if the grandmother was eaten by the wolf. Explain that this story is very old and that people have told it in many ways. In this story, the grandmother ran away and is safe from the wolf.

HELPING ATYPICAL LEARNERS

Disabled: Before children sequence the pictures, play back the story tape made in Lesson 14 or reread the story. (*Tape Recorder,* A-1) Display the letters A-G for visual learners when they do page 24.

Nonstandard English: Some speakers may use the double negative. ("She don't have no cape.") Model the standard usage for children to hear and repeat.

ADDITIONAL ACTIVITIES

Easy: Have children take turns acting out parts of "Little Red Riding Hood" as you retell the story. Be sure to use words that indicate the order in which the story events happened. (*first, next, then, last*)

Challenging: Have children work in three small groups. Divide a sheet of mural paper into three parts. Choose three main events from the story "Little Red Riding Hood." (Red Riding Hood meets the wolf; the wolf in bed talking to Red Riding Hood; the wolf running from Grandmother's house) Have each group choose one of these three scenes to illustrate. Talk about which picture will be first, next, last. Have groups illustrate the three scenes. Then ask children to retell the story using the finished mural.

This lesson is continued on the next page.

Telling a Story

ACTIVITY: telling what happened first, next, last in a story

OBJECTIVE: to recognize story sequence

TE 41

LESSON STEPS

- Have children look at page 24. Explain that it shows a picture that is not finished.

- Ask: "Who is the little girl in the picture?" (Little Red Riding Hood) "What part of the picture do you think is missing?" (cape or hood) Tell the children that to finish the picture they must connect the dots in order.

- Distribute red crayons. Have children find the capital letter *A* and draw a line to letter *B*. Check responses before having children draw a line from *B* to *C,* and so on.

- When children have completed the cape, have them begin at letter *A* and repeat the letters aloud, pointing to each letter.

ADDITIONAL ACTIVITIES

Easy: Have children take turns reciting the alphabet from *A* to *G*. Children may want to follow the letters on the cape.

Challenging: Use alphabet cards or write the alphabet on the chalkboard from *A* to *Z*. Separate the alphabet into segments: *A-G, H-N, O-U,* and *V-Z*. Then have children practice saying the letters in each segment.

TE 42

Following Directions

ACTIVITY: following letters in order to finish a picture   OBJECTIVE: to follow directions

OBJECTIVES
to identify pictured objects
to answer questions accurately
to recall details in a story

INSTRUCTIONAL VOCABULARY
second   fourth
third

ORAL VOCABULARY
answer   favorite

BASIC LESSON MATERIALS
none

LESSON STEPS

• Have children look at the pictures on page 25. Remind them of the story "Little Red Riding Hood." Ask them to point to and identify pictures that might be from that story. (Grandmother's house, wolf, wasp, woodsman, strawberries, cake, butter, Red Riding Hood) Say: "Look at the pictures in the first row (row 1). Find the house where Red Riding Hood's grandmother might live. Draw a circle around the house." Allow time for discussion about the farm house, the apartments, and the house in the woods.

This lesson is continued on the next page.

Telling a Story

1.

2.

3.

4.

ACTIVITY: circling pictures from the story "Little Red Riding Hood"

OBJECTIVE: to recall story details

TE 43

Lesson 16 (continued)

- Identify the pictures in the second row (row 2). (wolf, wasp, woodsman) Have children circle the picture that shows what made Grandmother run out of her house. (the wolf)

- Identify the pictures in the third row (row 3). Remind children to remember *all* the things Red Riding Hood brought. Ask: "What did Little Red Riding Hood bring to Grandmother? Draw a circle around the picture that shows all that she brought." (cake, butter, strawberries, flowers)

- Identify the pictures in the fourth row. Ask: "What made the wolf run away?" (the wasp) Have children circle the correct picture.

LISTENING/SPEAKING SKILLS

Review each row of pictures with the children. Ask why they did not choose the pictures that are not circled. Encourage children to use complete sentences when they answer. For the third row, remind children that some of the things Red Riding Hood brought Grandmother came from home, and that she picked the flowers in the woods.

HELPING ATYPICAL LEARNERS

Spanish Speaking: Give students questions to repeat so that they become familiar with the changed word order of questions. (*Repetition*)

ADDITIONAL ACTIVITIES

Easy: To provide further practice with recalling details, have children recall what happened in the nursery rhyme "Humpty Dumpty." Ask: "Where did Humpty Dumpty sit?" (on a wall) "What happened to him?" (He had a great fall.) "Who tried to put him together again?" (all the King's horses and all the King's men) "Could they put him together?" (no)

Challenging: Have children choose a part of the story "Little Red Riding Hood" that they liked best and illustrate that part of the story. When they have finished, have them share their drawings with the class. Encourage children to use complete sentences as they describe their illustrations.

17 | Talking about Why

OBJECTIVES
to observe, interpret, generalize about picture details
to participate in a group discussion
to understand cause and effect relationships

ORAL VOCABULARY
bulldozer   siren
engine   fire alarm

BASIC LESSON MATERIALS
none

LESSON STEPS

• Before beginning the lesson, talk about *why* some things happen. Tell the children they are to be detectives and pick out "clues" for the problems you will give them. Ask them what good detectives would know if they saw—

a wet umbrella, a raincoat, and rubbers in the hallway. (It is raining.)

a man with a paintbrush, a can, and a tall ladder. (He is probably going to paint.)

a girl with a large scrape on her knee and skates on her feet. (She fell down.)

This lesson is continued on the next page.

Talking about Why

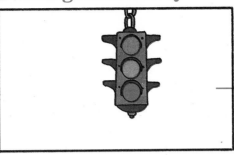

ACTIVITY: drawing lines from pictures that show what happened to pictures that show what caused it to happen

OBJECTIVE: to recognize cause and effect relationships

- Have children look at the pictures on page 26. Call attention to the picture of the cars stopped at the corner. Ask: "Why did the cars stop?" (The traffic light turned red.) Have children draw a line from the stopped cars to the traffic light.

- Have children look at the picture of the large plant with the flowers. Ask: "How did the plant grow so large?" (Someone took care of it.) Have children draw a line from the girl watering the plant to the picture of the large plant.

- Have children look at the picture of the birdhouse. Ask: "How do you think the birdhouse got up in the tree?" (Someone built and hung it.) Have them draw a line from the girl who is making the birdhouse to the picture of the finished birdhouse.

- Have children look at the pile of dirt next to the tall buildings. Ask: "What do you think made the pile of dirt?" (the bulldozer—a big strong machine that pushes piles of dirt) "Draw a line from the bulldozer to the picture of the pile of dirt."

ADDITIONAL ACTIVITIES

Easy: Give children the following "puzzles." Ask them to be good detectives and tell *why* things happened. Talk about the many possible answers to these puzzles. Sample answers are provided.

—The boy stayed in bed and did not go to school. (He was sick.)
—We smelled something delicious in the kitchen. (Someone was cooking.)
—The dog barked in the middle of the night. (He heard a noise.)

Challenging: Play a game called "Because." Give short, unfinished sentences that describe an action. Have children take turns finishing the sentences in their own words. Tell them that there are many possible answers.

I wrote a letter to my grandmother because _____. (she sent me a gift)
I made a birthday card for Dad because _____. (it was his birthday)
The girl ran to the bus stop because _____. (she was late)
Carol fixed a sandwich because _____. (she was hungry)

18 | Words That Tell About

LESSON STEPS

- Have children close their eyes and imagine a fire engine racing down the street. Ask what they hear. (siren) Have them imagine an ice cube. Ask how it feels. (cold) Have them imagine a large red apple. Ask how it tastes. (sweet) Have them imagine a pile of burning leaves. Ask what they smell. (smoke)

- Have children look at the row of pictures at the top of page 27. (hand, ear, nose, mouth) Explain that these are pictures of parts of our bodies that help us touch, hear, smell, and taste the things around us. Talk about the fact that we see things with our eyes, hear things with our ears, smell things with our noses, touch things with our hands, and taste things with our tongues.

This lesson is continued on the next two pages.

Words That Tell About

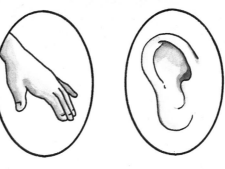
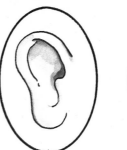
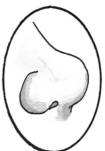
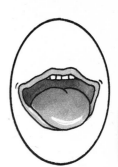

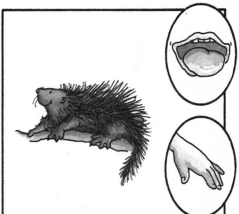

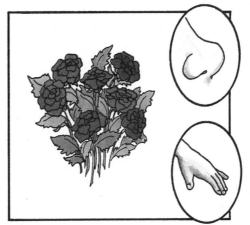

ACTIVITY: circling pictures of the parts of the body used to touch, hear, smell, and taste

OBJECTIVE: to recognize the touch, sound, smell, and taste associated with pictures

TE 47

Lesson 18 (continued)

- Have children look at the picture of the girl playing a drum. Talk about how we know some things without seeing them. "How do we know when a drum is being played?" (We hear it.) "Which part of the body do we use for hearing?" (ear) Have children circle the picture of the ear, because we can hear a drum being played. Ask children to think of words that tell how a drum sounds. (loud, banging, booming, rat-a-tat)

- Ask children what they know about a procupine. (It feels prickly.) Ask: "If you couldn't see the procupine, how would you know what animal it was?" (by touch) Have pupils circle the picture of the part of the body we use for touching things. (hand) Ask children to think of words that tell how a porcupine feels. (prickly, sharp, hard, rough)

- Ask children what they know about a rose. (It smells good.) Have them circle the picture of the part of the body we use for smelling things. (nose) Ask children to think of words that tell how roses smell. (good, sweet, flowery)

- Talk about the picture of the hamburger. Ask: "If you couldn't see the hamburger, how would you know what you were eating?" (by the taste) Have children circle the picture of the part of the body we use for tasting things. (mouth) Ask children to think of words that tell how a hamburger tastes (chewy, crispy, salty)

- Then have children look at page 28. Explain that each space contains a small picture. (nose, ear, hand, or mouth) In the space that has the picture of a nose, tell children to draw a picture of something they know by the way it smells. Follow a similar procedure for the remaining spaces.

LISTENING/SPEAKING SKILLS

Ask children to take turns describing something by the way it feels, looks, smells, sounds, or tastes. Have others guess what each child is describing.

HELPING ATYPICAL LEARNERS

Disabled: Do the Additional Activities first to establish a context for the lesson. (*Picture This*, V-2) Talk further about the senses by asking Yes-No questions, such as "Can you smell a flower?" or "Can you hear a doorbell?" (*Yes-No Questions*, D-1)

Spanish Speaking: Remind students that *who* is used for people and *what* is used for animals and things. Make up short sentences for students to turn into questions using *who* or *what*. For example: T—"My crayon is big." S—"What is big?" T—"My crayon." (*Question-Answer*)

Nonstandard English: Speakers of nonstandard English may omit the *-s* on the verb if the subject is singular. ("It feel cold." "That look burned.") Model standard usage for children to hear and repeat.

ADDITIONAL ACTIVITIES

Easy: Ask children to close their eyes and picture a kitchen. Have them pretend they are standing in the kitchen using their eyes, ears, noses, and hands. Ask: "What can you see? Can you hear something? What can you touch? What can you smell?"

Challenging: Play a game called "Mysteries." Ask the children to "solve" these mysteries. You might have children add more mysteries.

—It was very dark in the room, but I knew my dog was asleep beside my bed. How did I know? (touch, hearing)
—I had just opened the door, but I knew Mother was baking bread. How did I know? (smell)
—I was inside my house, but I knew it was snowing. How did I know? (sight)

Words That Tell About

Child will draw something they can smell here.

Child will draw something they can hear here.

Child will draw something they can touch here.

Child will draw something they can taste here.

ACTIVITY: drawing pictures of things we smell, hear, touch, and taste

OBJECTIVE: to associate the senses with everyday experiences

19 | Big, Medium, Little

OBJECTIVES
- to compare and match objects by size
- to understand the terms *big, medium, little*
- to create original art

INSTRUCTIONAL VOCABULARY
big   little
medium   middle

BASIC LESSON MATERIALS
paste
scissors

LESSON STEPS
- Have children recall and imagine the three bears from the story "Goldilocks." Tell them to show with their hands and arms the great big bear, the medium-sized bear, and the little baby bear. (arms open wide or hands together) You might suggest other comparisons for children to show with their hands and arms. (baby, 10-year-old, grown-up)

- Have children look at page 29. Point out the sizes of the three doghouses. Ask children to find the big one. Say: "Put your finger on it. Now find the little one and put your finger on it." Check responses to see that children understand. Finally ask: "Which one is medium-sized?" (the doghouse in the middle)

TE 50

Big, Medium, Little

blue
doghouse
here

red
doghouse
here

yellow
doghouse
here

ACTIVITY: talking about big, medium, and little   OBJECTIVE: to identify big, medium, and little

VISUAL SKILLS: Matching Sizes   **29**

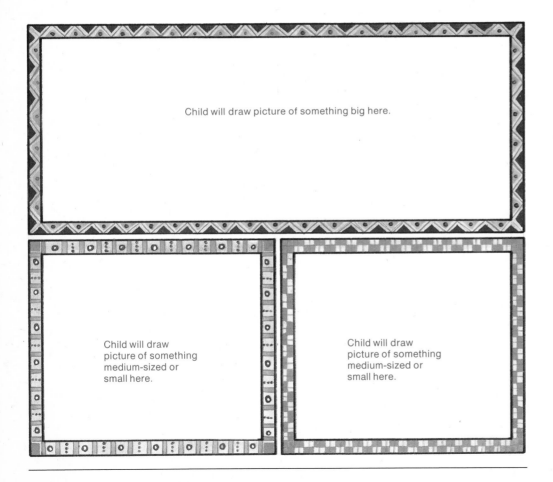

Child will draw picture of something big here.

Child will draw picture of something medium-sized or small here.

Child will draw picture of something medium-sized or small here.

- Next have children talk about the dogs. Have them point to the big, little, and medium-sized dogs. Ask children which dog they think fits into which doghouse. Ask how they know. (The big dog fits in the big doghouse, and so on.)

- Distribute blunt scissors and paste. Remind children to use scissors carefully. Supervise their work. Tell them that they will find the right doghouse for each dog and paste it below the dog. Have children cut out the three doghouses and place each in the correct space below the dog. Check responses before children paste.

- Have children look at the three spaces for drawing on page 30. Talk about things that are big, medium-sized, and little. Suggest things in the classroom that are often three sizes. (blocks, trucks, chalk, pencil, books) Have children draw a picture of something big in the large space at the top of the page. In the remaining boxes, have them draw pictures of something medium-sized and something little.

This lesson is continued on the next page.

Lesson 19 (continued)

LISTENING/SPEAKING SKILLS

Have children take turns describing the three items they drew on page 30. Encourage them to use the words *big, medium-sized,* and *little.*

HELPING ATYPICAL LEARNERS

Disabled: Do the Additional Activities first to establish a context for the lesson. Before children do page 30, help them to generate a list of medium-sized and little objects. (*Class Examples,* D-3)

Spanish Speaking: Use the *Question-Answer* format to provide practice in using adjectives. For example, hold up a book and say, "Tell me about the book." Students respond in complete sentences: "The book is little."

ADDITIONAL ACTIVITIES

Easy: Display a golf ball, a tennis ball or softball, and a volley ball or basketball. Talk about the sizes and have children take turns putting the balls in order while using the terms *big, medium-sized,* and *little.* On the chalkboard, draw three circles, three squares, and a three rectangles. Draw a big, a medium-sized, and a little shape. Have children take turns pointing to the medium-sized circle, the big rectangle, and so on.

Challenging: Read the story "Goldilocks and the Three Bears." Have children draw bowls, chairs, and beds for the little, medium-sized, and big bears in the story. Have children take turns telling parts of the story and using their drawings to illustrate the retelling.

20 Alike and Different

OBJECTIVES
to classify objects by function
to identify similar characteristics
to follow directions

ORAL VOCABULARY
vacuum cleaner

BASIC LESSON MATERIALS
none

LESSON STEPS

- Have children look at row 1 on page 31. Help them name the pictures. Ask: "What is the same about a car, bus, and a truck?" (They all have wheels, and can take someone or something from one place to another.) "Can a house take you somewhere?" (no) "Then which of these does not belong with the other? Why not?" (the house; it cannot take you somewhere) Have children mark an X on the house.

- Help children name the pictures in row 2. (broom, cup and saucer, vacuum cleaner, mop) Ask the children to name things that might be used for cleaning. (broom, mop, vacuum cleaner) Ask: "Which does not belong with the others? Why?" (cup and saucer; not used for cleaning) Have children mark an X on the cup and saucer.

This lesson is continued on the next page.

Alike and Different

1.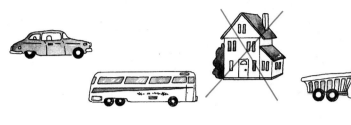

2.

3.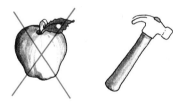

4.

ACTIVITY: marking an X on pictures that do not belong in the group

OBJECTIVE: to understand how to group things with similar characteristics

TE 53

Lesson 20 (continued)

- Help name the pictures in row 3. (apple, hammer, screwdriver, and wrench) Ask: "Why do the hammer, screw driver, and wrench belong together?" (They are all tools.) "Which picture does not belong, and why?" (apple; not a tool) Have children mark an *X* on the apple.

- Help children name the pictures in row 4. (banana, ear of corn, carrot, cat) Ask: "Why do the banana, corn, and carrot belong together?" (They are all food.) "Which picture does not belong, and why?" (the cat; not something to eat) Have children mark an *X* on the cat.

LISTENING/SPEAKING SKILLS

Look at page 31 again. Have the children take turns talking about how items are alike and how they are different. Encourage such responses from the children as: "This bus is like the car because . . ." "The house is not like the truck because . . ." Remind children to use complete sentences.

ADDITIONAL ACTIVITIES

Easy: Have children use pictures to label three envelopes: food, clothing, vehicles. You might write: *Things We Eat; Things We Wear; Things That Go.* Read the labels for the children. Have them search through used magazines for pictures, or draw their own, of things to go in each of the envelopes. After several pictures are in each envelope, check responses. Then remove the pictures, place them in a random display, and have children work in pairs to put the pictures back in the appropriate envelopes. Have them talk about their choices.

Challenging: Choose several items that have a common characteristic. Point them out to the children and ask them to identify how the items are the same. Some suggestions include: chair, sofa, bench (things you sit on); milk, juice, water (things you drink); piano, drum, horn (things that make music); duck, cat, elephant (animals). You might ask children to take turns suggesting groups of items that are similar.

21 Listening to a Story

OBJECTIVES

to sequence a series of events
to recall story events not pictured
to discuss differences in abilities,
    skills, talents of individuals

ORAL VOCABULARY

broad bill	scoop
pointed beak	scatter
sunflower seeds	scrambled
web	furiously
eggshell	sprawl
nibble	stubby
tumble	rooster
peck	hatch

BASIC LESSON MATERIALS

paste
scissors

LESSON STEPS

- See the story "Skip and Waddle," Resource Unit, page TE 106–TE 107.

- Tell children they will hear a story about a duckling and a chicken. Ask them to listen to find out how the animals are alike and how they are different. Read the story "Skip and Waddle" aloud.

This lesson is continued on the next two pages.

Listening to a Story

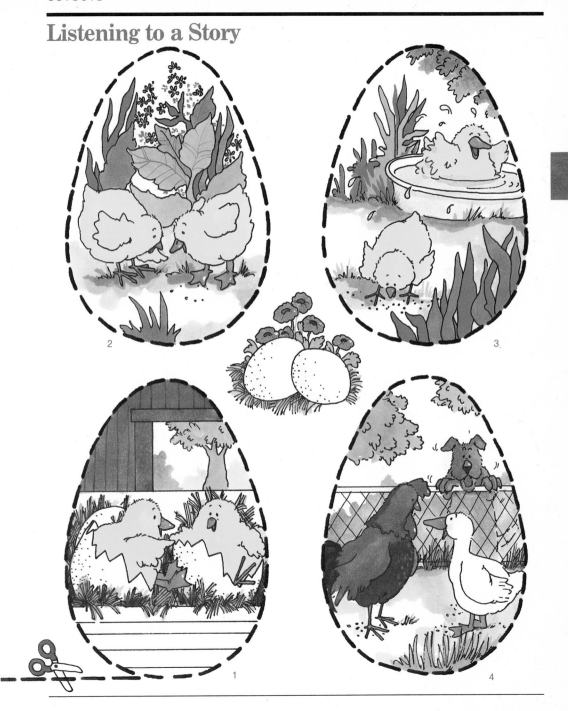

Lesson 21 (continued)

- Talk about the story with the children. Compare the duckling and the chick. Ask: "How are they the same? How are they different?" (*Alike:* both came from eggs, both were small and yellow, both liked to eat, sleep, and play. *Different:* duckling had a broad bill for scooping his food, chick had a little pointed beak; duckling had webs between his toes, chick had long slim toes; duckling's feathers were white, chick's were red and brown.)

- Distribute blunt scissors and paste. Carefully supervise the children's use of scissors and paste.

- Ask children to look at the pictures on page 32. Say: "Find the picture that shows what happened first in the story." (chick and duckling hatching)

- Now have the children look at the spaces on page 33. Point out that the spaces are numbered 1, 2, 3, and 4. Explain that they will cut out the picture that shows what happened first and paste it in the space that is numbered 1. Have the children cut out the picture of the chick and duckling hatching and paste it in place. Follow a similar procedure as each picture is identified.

- Next help the children find the picture that shows what happened second (Waddle wanted to swim and Skip wanted to scratch), third (Waddle and Skip discover that their feet are different), and fourth (the black dog frightens them into giving their grown-up calls, "cock-a-doodle-doo" and "quack-quack"). You might need to reread parts of the story as the children sequence the pictures.

- Ask: "What do Skip and Waddle learn at the end of the story?" (that they are different animals)

- When the children have completed page 33, ask them to take turns telling parts of the story "Skip and Waddle" using the pictures as aids.

HELPING ATYPICAL LEARNERS
Disabled: Record the story of "Skip and Waddle" as you read it. (*Tape Recorder,* A-1) Children work in pairs to discuss likenesses and differences. (*Student-Pair Dialogue,* A-2a) Play back the story as children arrange the pictures on page 33 in the correct sequence.

ADDITIONAL ACTIVITIES
Easy: Play a game called "Skip or Waddle?" Read the following statements and ask "Who am I, Skip or Waddle?"

—I have a pointed beak and I peck for food. (Skip)
—I have skin called webs between my toes. (Waddle)
—I like to swim. (Waddle)
—I like to scratch for food. (Skip)
—I say "quack-quack." (Waddle)
—I say "cock-a-doodle-doo." (Skip)
—I am a duck (Waddle)
—I am a chicken. (Skip)

Challenging: Talk about how each of us is different from others. Discuss things individual children do well. Be sure to include something each child does well. Have children tell something they would like to do when they grow up. Talk about how people with different talents are needed in the world.

Listening to a Story

1.

2.

3.

4.

ACTIVITY: placing story pictures in correct order   OBJECTIVE: to recognize a sequence of story events

TE 57

OBJECTIVES

to recall details in a story
to identify colors: red, blue, brown, black, white, purple
to answer questions accurately

INSTRUCTIONAL VOCABULARY

red	black
blue	white
brown	purple

BASIC LESSON MATERIALS

LESSON STEPS

Note: The instructional vocabulary listed may require specific preteaching. Suggestions are included here as part of the Lesson Steps.

- Briefly review the story "Skip and Waddle." Have children look at the pictures on page 34. Help them identify the rooster (Skip) and the duck (Waddle). Point out that Skip is the red and brown animal and that Waddle is the white animal. Reinforce the understanding that Skip is a chicken and Waddle is a duck.

- Explain that children will answer questions about Skip and Waddle by circling the correct animal. Tell them that they can find the right box by finding the right colored egg. Ask children to point to the black egg, the brown egg, the purple egg. Check responses as children locate the boxes.

- Say: "Now we are ready to do the page. Listen carefully to the directions. Put your finger on the black egg. Draw a circle around the animal in that box that can say, 'cock-a-doodle-do.' " (Skip)

- "Put your finger on the white egg. Draw a circle around the animal that has a pointed beak." (Skip)

- "Put your finger on the blue egg. Draw a circle around the animal in that box that can say, 'quack, quack.' " (Waddle)

- "Put your finger on the brown egg. Draw a circle around the animal that can scratch for worms." (Skip)

- "Put your finger on the purple egg. Draw a circle around the animal that has skin between its toes." (Waddle)

- "Put your finger on the red egg. Draw a circle around the animal that likes to swim." (Waddle)

LISTENING/SPEAKING SKILLS

Have children take turns answering the same questions orally. ("Which animal has a pointed beak?") Encourage them to answer in complete sentences. ("Skip is a chicken. Chickens have pointed beaks.")

HELPING ATYPICAL LEARNERS

Disabled: Play *Simon Says* with students, stressing color identification. For example, say, "Simon says clap your hands when I point to something brown." (*Play-Off,* D-2) Children who have a problem recalling story details should listen again to the tape made in Lesson 21.

Spanish-Speaking: To help build vocabulary, have each student name three things different animals can do. (example: *quack, swim, peck*)

ADDITIONAL ACTIVITIES

Easy: Have children take turns pointing to pictures of Skip or Waddle on page 34 and telling something about the animal. (Skip is a chicken. Waddle is a duck. Skip has a pointed beak. Waddle has white feathers, and so on.)

Challenging: Have children work in pairs and make up riddles about Skip or Waddle. (I scoop up my food; I can swim; who am I? I have webbed feet; I say, "quack, quack"; who am I?) As children gain practice making up riddles, encourage them to make clues less obvious. Have children present their riddles to others to answer.

Answering Questions

ACTIVITY: circling pictures that answer questions about a story

OBJECTIVE: to recall story details

34   LANGUAGE SKILLS: Recalling Details

Alike and Different

LESSON STEPS

• Ask children to pretend they are holding something imaginary in their hands as you tell them what to hold. Encourage them to pantomime holding the objects. (a kitten, a puppy, a giraffe) Ask children what is the same about a kitten, a dog, and a giraffe. (They are all animals.) What animal is really different from the others? (The giraffe, because it is bigger.)

• Have children look at the rows of pictures on page 35. For row 1, help children name the pictures. (squirrel, rabbit, bear, cat) Ask: "How are these things alike?" (They are all animals.) "Can you find one animal that is different from the rest?" (bear) "How is the bear different?" (It is bigger.) Have children mark an *X* on the bear. Follow a similar procedure for the remaining rows.

• *Row 2:* three one-family homes and a skyscraper apartment building. All these pictures show buildings where people live. The skyscraper is different because it is bigger and is the home of many families. Have children mark an *X* on the apartment building.

• *Row 3:* tricycle, bicycle, bus, motorcycle. All these pictures show things that people ride. The bus is much bigger and carries many people, not just one rider. Have children mark an *X* on the bus.

• *Row 4:* bee, fly, airplane, bird. All these pictures show things that fly. The airplane does not belong because it is much bigger. It is not alive. It needs an engine to make it fly. Have children mark an *X* on the airplane.

HELPING ATYPICAL LEARNERS

Disabled: Give extra examples similar to those on page 35 for children to do with you. (*Teacher-Student Dialogue,* A-2b)

Nonstandard English: Some speakers may use the construction "more bigger." Model standard usage for children to hear and repeat.

ADDITIONAL ACTIVITIES

Easy: From magazines or seed catalogs, cut pictures of flowers, bushes, and trees. Have children select examples of each type to paste on a chart to be called "Different Kinds of Plants." Talk about the fact that all are plants, but that trees usually grow much bigger than other plants.

Challenging: Have children look in books and magazines for different kinds of buildings. Encourage them to show the pictures to others and to classify the buildings. (school, office, home, hospital, factory) Encourage children to think of different kinds of buildings in your city or town and to describe them by size and use.

Alike and Different

1.

2.

3.

4.

ACTIVITY: marking an *X* on pictures that do not belong in the group

OBJECTIVE: to understand how to group things by size

TE 61

From Ginn English Program Grade K, copyrighted by Ginn and Company.

VISUAL SKILLS: Telling Alike and Different 35

OBJECTIVES
to listen to a poem
to distinguish reality from fantasy
to pantomime a story poem

ORAL VOCABULARY

elf	tug
dormouse	topple
toadstool	gracious
week	lament
shelter	invent
heap	

BASIC LESSON MATERIALS
scissors
tape

LESSON STEPS
- See the poem "The Elf and the Dormouse," Resource Unit, page TE 107.

- Talk about things that are real and things that are make-believe. (*make-believe:* dogs that talk, elves, Little Red Riding Hood; *real:* teachers, dogs that bark, children who go to kindergarten) Explain that some things we read about are make-believe. The people and places in these stories are not real and the things that happen could not happen in real life. Tell children that the poem they will hear is just such a make-believe story. Ask them to listen carefully to find out what happens. Ask them to listen especially to hear how umbrellas were invented.

CUTOUTS

Listening to a Poem

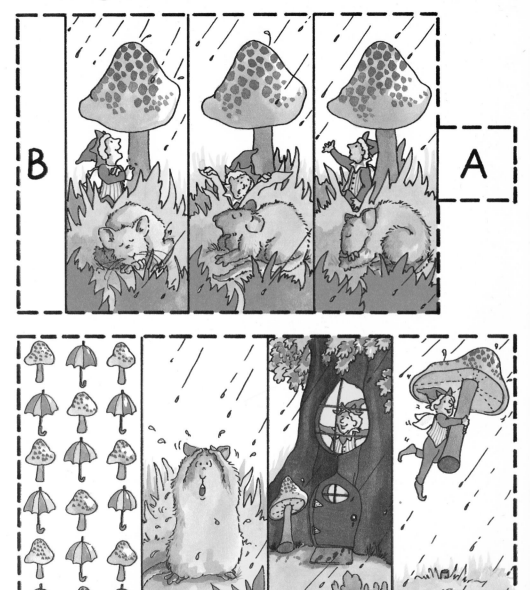

ACTIVITY: to listen to a poem

OBJECTIVE: to listen to and recall poem details

Listening to a Poem

- Read the poem "The Elf and the Dormouse" aloud. Talk about the story the poem tells. After you have read the poem ask: "What did the wee elf use for an umbrella?" (a toadstool) Talk about how this could not really happen in real life.

- Have the children look at the picture strips on page 36. Explain that the pictures show parts of what happened in the poem, and that when they are pasted together the strips make a "show" to slide through the slits in a make-believe stage.

- Distribute blunt scissors. Remind the children to use scissors carefully. Supervise as children cut out the two strips on page 36. Help them tape the strips together to form one continuous strip. (Tape tab B under the strip at the picture of the elf flying away with the toadstool.)

- Have children find the stage on pages 37–38 and cut on the dashed lines. You may wish to cut the slits on the dashed lines within each stage, for sliding the picture strips through. Show the children how to insert the strips at tab A and how to slide the strips through the stage.

- Reread the poem as children slide the strips through. Stop and talk about each picture as it appears on the stage. Tell children when to change pictures.

     Picture 1—The elf finds shelter under a toadstool.
     Picture 2—Elf discovers Dormouse.
     Picture 3—Elf has an idea about how to get home without getting wet.

This lesson is continued on the next page.

From Ginn English Program Grade K, copyrighted by Ginn and Company.   LANGUAGE SKILLS: Talking about a Poem 37

TE 63

Lesson 24 (continued)

Picture 4—Elf flies home under his "umbrella."

Picture 5—Elf is home safe and dry.

Picture 6—Dormouse wakes up to find the shelter gone.

LISTENING/SPEAKING SKILLS

Reread the poem and have children listen and talk about the parts of the poem that could be real (toadstool, dormouse, rainy day) and the parts that are make-believe. (elf using a toadstool as an umbrella, a talking dormouse, the idea that an elf invented umbrellas). Have children pantomime the actions of the elf and the dormouse as you read the poem.

HELPING ATYPICAL LEARNERS

Disabled: Make a tape as you read the poem. Children listen several times with eyes closed before making the strips for the puppet stage. (*Picture This,* V-2) Offer help as necessary for the cut-and-paste activity. (*Fine-Motor SOS,* D-4)

Nonstandard English: As children tell the actions, watch for lack of agreement of subject and verb. ("The elf fly.") Model standard usage for children to hear and repeat.

ADDITIONAL ACTIVITIES

Easy: If possible, tape record the poem "The Elf and the Dormouse." Encourage children to listen to the tape and follow along with their picture strips.

Challenging: Have children retell the story "The Elf and the Dormouse" in their own words as they use their strips and stage. Encourage them to take the stage home and retell the story.

Listening to a Poem

25 | Inside or Outside?

OBJECTIVES
   to classify objects by location
     (inside—outside)
   to observe, interpret, generalize
     about pictured items
   to follow directions

ORAL VOCABULARY
   fire hydrant   bureau

BASIC LESSON MATERIALS
   none

LESSON STEPS

- Tell children to look at the pictures in the rows on page 39. Help them name the pictures in row 1. (lawn mower, toaster, TV, telephone) For each picture, ask: "Where is it used, inside or outside?" Explain that in this row, most of the things are used inside the house. Have children find the thing that is used outside the house and mark an *X* on it. (lawn mower)

- Help the children name the pictures in row 2. (fire hydrant, lamp pole, traffic light, kitchen clock) For each picture, ask: "Where is it used, inside or outside?" Explain that in this row most of the things are used outside the house. Have children find the thing that is used inside the house and mark an *X* on it. (kitchen clock)

This lesson is continued on the next page.

Inside or Outside?

1.

2.

3.

4.

ACTIVITY: marking an *X* on pictures that do not belong in the group

OBJECTIVE: to understand how to group things by location

VISUAL SKILLS: Telling Alike and Different **39**

Lesson 25 (continued)

- Help children name the pictures in row 3. (bed, fire hydrant, bunk beds, bureau or chest of drawers) For each picture, ask: "Where is it used, inside or outside?" Then ask where *most* of the things in this row are used. (inside) Have children find the thing that is used outside the house and mark an *X* on it. (fire hydrant)

- Help children name the pictures in row 4. (moon, rocket ship, chair, sun) For each picture, ask: "Where would you find it, inside or outside the house?" Then ask where *most* of the things in this row are found. (outside) Have children find the thing that is usually found inside the house and mark an *X* on it. (chair)

LISTENING/SPEAKING SKILLS

Review the page. Have children take turns talking about why they marked an *X* on a picture. Encourage them to use complete sentences. ("The lawn mower is used outside.")

HELPING ATYPICAL LEARNERS

Disabled: Tell children, "Simon says point out the window when you hear something that is used outside." Use a similar procedure for inside objects. (*Play-Off,* D-2) Point out that some objects can be used inside and outside. Children should indicate where the object is used more often.

ADDITIONAL ACTIVITIES

Easy: Help children dictate a list of things that are used inside the house and a list of things used outside. Suggest additions to the completed lists, asking in which list they should be placed and why. (Suggestions for additions might include kites, desk, plates, tree house, umbrella, toothbrush, mailbox.)

Challenging: Have children fold a sheet of paper in half. On the inside of the paper, have them draw an "inside picture" (something that is used inside the house) and on the outside an "outside picture" (something used outside). Have them explain their pictures to others.

26

Where Does It Belong?

OBJECTIVES

- to use appropriate words to identify and describe directional relationships
- to discuss vehicles, buildings, and transportation
- to relate objects to an appropriate environment

INSTRUCTIONAL VOCABULARY

in front of	above
behind	below

ORAL VOCABULARY

country	briefcase

BASIC LESSON MATERIALS

- paste
- scissors

LESSON STEPS

- Review directional words with the children. Help them locate classroom objects by using the words *top, middle, bottom, in front of, behind, above, below.*

- Have children look at the pictures on page 40. Name the pictures with the children. (tractor, cow, chickens, farmer, bus, stop sign, fire hydrant, woman) Ask where they would find each thing in the picture—in the city or on a farm. Talk about why some things could be found in both places.

This lesson is continued on the next two pages.

CUTOUTS

Where Does It Belong?

Child will paste these pictures on appropriate scenes on page 41.

Lesson 26 (continued)

- Have the children look at page 41. "What things do you see in the top picture?" (farmyard with house and barn) "What things do you see in the bottom picture?" (city street, shoe store, flower shop, cat) Help children conclude that at the top of the page is a picture of a farm and at the bottom is a picture of a city street.

- Tell the children to decide where each thing pictured on page 40 should be placed, on the farm or on the city street. Talk about each picture. Ask: "What pictures will you put on the farm?" (tractor, cow, chicken, farmer) "What pictures will you put on the city street?" (bus, stop sign, fire hydrant, woman) Talk about the man and woman in the pictures. Ask how the children know the man belongs in the farm picture and the woman belongs in the city picture. (clothing)

- Have children cut out pictures on page 40 and paste them in the correct picture on page 41. Remind children to be careful when using scissors and paste.

Where Does It Belong?

ACTIVITY: placing pictures where they belong on the farm or in the city

OBJECTIVE: to relate pictures to an appropriate setting

LISTENING/SPEAKING SKILLS

Have children take turns talking about where they pasted each picture. Encourage them to use direction words such as *in front of, between, behind, on top of, under.*

EXTRA INFORMATION

Borrow a filmstrip or several books about farm and city life. Talk about farms and farm equipment. Help the children understand that a farm is a place where food is grown. Explain that in the city people buy the food raised on farms.

HELPING ATYPICAL LEARNERS

Disabled: Play *Simon Says* (*Play-Off,* D-2) to practice the Instructional Vocabulary. ("Simon says stand in front of your chair.") Be available to help with the cut-and-paste activity. (*Fine-Motor SOS,* D-4) Provide picture books for children unfamiliar with city or country objects.

Nonstandard English: Provide a model of the standard usage of the verb *be* if children use nonstandard usage. ("I be living on a farm.")

ADDITIONAL ACTIVITIES

Easy: Display several pictures of different environments from books or magazines. Ask questions about the pictures. "Where would you see this? When? At any special time of day? How often would you see it? How do you know?" You might hold up a picture of cars on a highway. Children might say that they see cars on streets in the city or on country roads. You might point out that there are more cars on city streets in mornings and late afternoons when people go to and from work. Encourage children to speak in complete sentences.

Challenging: Prepare a display called "Where Is It?" Cut several interesting pictures from used magazines. Ask children to describe the pictures by using such sentences as "The fish is in the water." "The child is on a horse." "The dog is in a bedroom." Encourage different responses by telling the children that there is no "right" answer.

27

Using a Calendar

Using a Calendar

OBJECTIVES
to observe and discuss the weather
to observe and discuss a calendar
to recognize and associate weather
symbols

BASIC LESSON MATERIALS
none

LESSON STEPS

- It is best to begin this lesson on a Monday so that the children can talk about and record the weather each day for a week.

- Have the children look at page 42. Ask: "What is a calendar for?" (It helps us keep track of days and dates.) Explain that calendars show the days of the week and the date of each day.

- Point to and read the names of days of the week. Have children repeat them as you read them a second time. Count the days of the week with the children. Tell them that calendars can be used as reminders of what happened each day.

- Have children look at page 43. Help them point to and recognize each picture or symbol. (*sun*—a sunny day; *cloud with sun peeking out*—a cloudy or partly cloudy day; *face blowing wind*—a windy day; *cloud with rain or snow falling*—rainy or snowy day)

Sunday

Monday

Tuesday

Wednesday

Thursday

Friday

Saturday

ACTIVITY: making a weather chart; using a calendar   OBJECTIVE: to observe and record the weather; to recognize the function of a calendar

Talking about the Weather

Child will circle appropriate weather symbols for each day of the week.

ACTIVITY: talking about the weather   OBJECTIVE: to observe the weather

- Talk about the weather each day for a week. Then opposite the correct day of the week, circle the picture(s) or symbol(s) describing the day's weather.

- In the space next to the name of each day, children may wish to draw a picture of something they did that day.

LISTENING / SPEAKING SKILLS

Have children take turns using their calendars to tell something about the weather and what they did at school that day. Encourage the use of complete sentences. ("On Monday it was rainy. We played a game in school.")

This lesson is continued on the next page.

TE 71

Lesson 27 (continued)

HELPING ATYPICAL LEARNERS

Disabled: Provide extended practice in saying the days of the week. Put the days on tape for auditory learners.

Spanish Speaking: The days of the week are not capitalized in Spanish.

Nonstandard English: Provide oral practice with past tense verbs to help children use the -*ed* ending. ("On Monday we worked in the classroom.")

ADDITIONAL ACTIVITIES

Easy: Encourage children to look closely at the sky and become aware of how the air feels and how cold or warm it is. Then have them choose the appropriate pictures or symbols for the weather from the chart.

Reread the poem "The Elf and the Dormouse." Ask "Which weather picture or symbol would go with this story?" (rain)

Challenging: Have children make a weather booklet. Ask them to draw their own weather pictures, one on each page of the booklet. Then have them think of words that describe the weather represented by each picture. *(bright, sunny, windy, cool, breezy, cloudy, warm)* Write the words on the chalkboard and have children copy the words in their booklets on the appropriate pages.

This cutouts page will be used with Lesson 29 (see pages TE 79–TE 81). Have students skip this page for now.

Listening to a Story

The Tale of

Title

Peter Rabbit

cover picture

Child will paste these pictures and those on pages 46 and 48 in sequence on pages 49 and 50 to make a book.

ACTIVITY: listening to story "The Tale of Peter Rabbit"   OBJECTIVE: to listen to and recall story details

OBJECTIVES

to discriminate picture details visually

to recognize variations in two details; three details

to recognize similarities in pictured items

ORAL VOCABULARY

scarecrow	tool shed
mischief	cucumber
hoe	vine
blackberry	gooseberry
naughty	cabbage
disobey	whisker
parsley	

BASIC LESSON MATERIALS

LESSON STEPS

- See the story "The Tale of Peter Rabbit" in the Resource Unit, page TE 108.

- If possible, tape record the story and have it available to the children for frequent listening. Tell children that they will hear a story about a naughty little bunny. Ask them to listen to see what happens to him. Read the story "The Tale of Peter Rabbit" aloud. Tell children that they will skip some pages in their books, but assure them that they will come back and complete the work at a later time.

- Have the children turn to page 45 and look at the pictures. Remind them of the part of the story in which Peter went into Mr. Mc-Gregor's garden to eat the farmer's vegetables. Talk about how Peter was dressed. Tell the children that Peter looked like the first picture in row 1. (Peter with jacket and a carrot) Then say: "Now find a picture in row 1 that shows Peter looking just like the first picture in the row." (picture 4) Talk about the differences in picture detail. (In the second picture, Peter has no jacket. In the third, Peter has no carrot.) Have children circle the last picture in the row.

- Identify Mr. McGregor in row 2. Have children talk about the first picture. (Farmer McGregor with hat and rake) Ask them to find the picture in row 2 that shows Mr. Mc-Gregor looking just the same as the first picture. (picture 2) Talk about how the other pictures of Mr. McGregor are different. (picture 3, no rake; picture 4, no hat) Have children circle picture 2.

- In row 3, talk about the first picture. (Mother Rabbit with basket and hat) Tell children to find the picture in the row that shows Mother Rabbit looking the same as the first picture. (picture 3) Talk about how the other pictures are different. (picture 2, no hat; picture 4, no basket) Have children circle picture 3.

- Before going to row 4, talk about a scarecrow. Ask why farmers use scarecrows. (to scare away the birds or animals that might eat the farmer's vegetables) Have children describe the first picture. (scarecrow with hat, coat, and tie) Have them find the picture in row 4 that looks the same. (picture 2) Talk about how each of the other pictures is different. (picture 3, no tie; picture 4, no hat) Ask children to circle picture 2.

- Although this lesson continues on text page 47, you may wish to break it at this point, completing page 47 in another session. Additional Activities are provided for each session.

- Should you wish to complete the lesson in one session, continue with the Lesson Steps on page TE 76.

HELPING ATYPICAL LEARNERS

Disabled: Tape-record "The Tale of Peter Rabbit" as you read it. (*Tape Recorder*, A-1) Children listen to the story a second time with eyes closed. (*Picture This*, V-2) Auditory and visual learners work in pairs to do page 45. Check the progress of each pair. (*Teacher Float*, V-3; *Student-Pair Dialogue*, A-2a)

ADDITIONAL ACTIVITIES

Easy: On the chalkboard draw two rows of four circles each. With colored chalk draw two details (lines, dots, or zigzags) on the first circle in each row. Repeat this design on one of the other circles in the row. Have children identify the circles in each row with the same designs.

Challenging: Ask children to draw pictures of Peter Rabbit as he appears in different parts of the story. (with or without his shoes or jacket) Have others take turns describing the differences they see.

This lesson is continued on the next three pages.

Alike and Different

ACTIVITY: circling pictures that look like the first picture in the row

OBJECTIVE: to recognize pictures that are alike and different

TE 75

From Ginn English Program Grade K, copyrighted by Ginn and Company.

VISUAL SKILLS: Telling Alike and Different **45**

Lesson 28 (continued)

LESSON STEPS

- Next have children turn to page 47. Remind them that they will complete page 46 later. Explain that on page 47, children will be looking again for the picture that looks like the first picture in the row. On this page, however, they will have to look a little harder to find the one that looks the same.

- Talk about the first picture in row 1. (white cat with both ears up, tail curled to right) Say: "Tell how the other pictures are different." (picture 2, left ear down; picture 3, tail curled to the left) Have children circle picture 4.

- In row 2, identify Flopsy for the children. Talk about the way Flopsy is dressed. (dress with collar, bow, long sleeves) Ask children to find the picture in which Flopsy's dress is the same as the first picture (picture 3) Ask how the other pictures are different. (picture 2, no collar; picture 1, no bow) Tell children to circle the picture that looks the same. (picture 3)

- Have children talk about and describe the first picture in row 3. (mouse with bean in its mouth, long tail, large ears) Have them find the picture in the row that looks just the same. (picture 2) Ask: "How are the other pictures different?" (picture 3, no tail; picture 4, no ears)

Listening to a Story

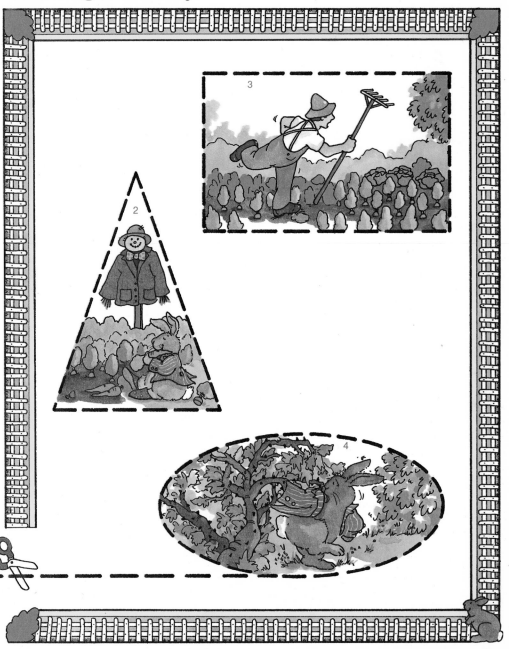

Alike and Different

1.

2.

3.

4.

ACTIVITY: circling pictures that look like the first picture in the row

OBJECTIVE: to recognize pictures that are alike and different

From Ginn English Program Grade K, copyrighted by Ginn and Company.

VISUAL SKILLS: Telling Alike and Different   47

- Have children identify and describe the first picture in row 4. (Peter with ears flopping, whiskers, and a tail) Ask them to find the picture that looks just the same. (picture 3) Ask how the other pictures are different. (picture 2, only one ear flopping; last picture 4, no whiskers) Tell children to circle the picture that looks the same. (picture 3)

ADDITIONAL ACTIVITIES

Easy: Have children look in used magazines for pictures of three cats and three dogs, all different. Help them cut out the pictures and mount them on construction paper. Then talk about the likenesses and differences in the pictures.

Challenging: Have children return to page 47 and identify the pictures of the story characters from "The Tale of Peter Rabbit." Have them point to the first picture in each row and talk about what is happening in each picture, referring to the event in the story. You might reread the story or have children listen again to the tape recording.

TE 77

Lesson 28 (continued)

This cutouts page will be used with Lesson 29 (see pages TE 79–TE 81). Have students skip this page for now.

Listening to a Story

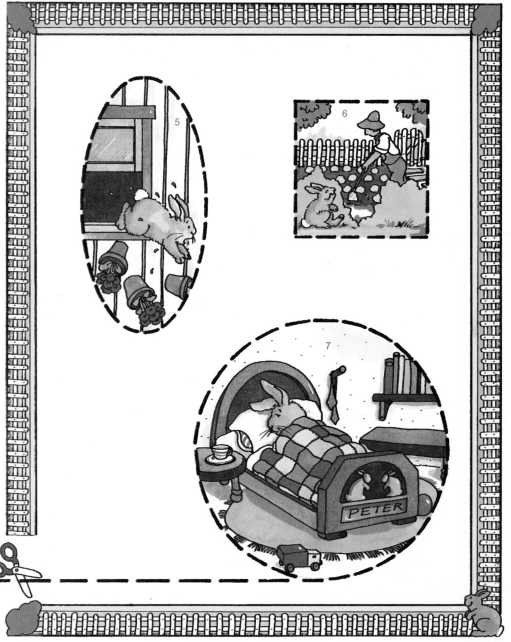

Listening to a Story

OBJECTIVES
to identify story details
to recognize the sequence of story
events
to match similar shapes

ORAL VOCABULARY
book title   The End
cover

BASIC LESSON MATERIALS
paste
scissors

LESSON STEPS

Note: This lesson is the culmination of the Peter Rabbit sequence. As such, students will be using cutouts pages 44, 46, 48, 49, and 50 to create their booklets.

• Have children turn to page 44. Point to and read the story title, "The Tale of Peter Rabbit." Explain that the title is the name of the story. Tell the children that the big picture under the title will be put on the cover of a little book they will make. The small picture will be the first one inside the little book. Talk about the small picture. (Mrs. Rabbit and her four children) Explain that this picture will be first in the little book because it shows the Rabbit family before Peter's adventures begin.

This lesson is continued on the next two pages.

Listening to a Story

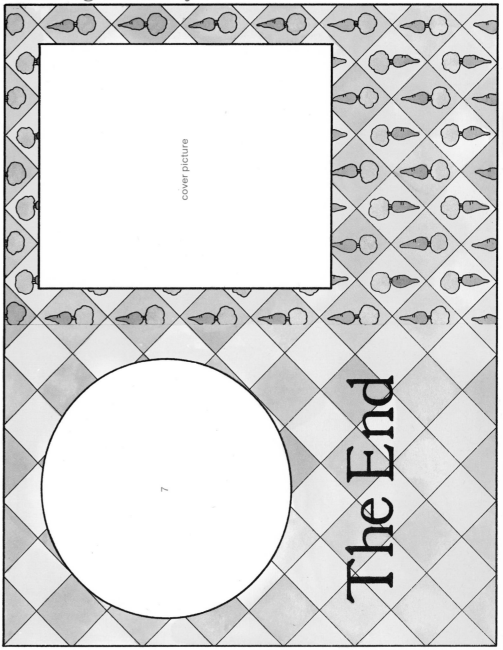

cover picture

7

The End

ACTIVITY: listening to a story

OBJECTIVE: to listen to and recall story details

Lesson 29 (continued)

- Have children turn to page 46. Explain that the pictures on the page tell the story just the way the story happened.

- Talk about each picture. Use words that describe story order. (*first, next, then, last*)

  Top left—Peter eating the vegetables in Mr. McGregor's garden

  Top right—Peter holding his stomach, because he ate too much

  Bottom left—Mr. McGregor chasing Peter with a rake

  Bottom right—Peter, without shoes, stuck in the bushes

- Next, have children turn to page 48 and talk about the remaining pictures.

  Top left—Peter jumping out of the window of the tool shed, upsetting the pots

  Top right—Peter meeting the mouse and the white cat

  Bottom left—Peter about to dash past Mr. McGregor to reach the gate

  Bottom right—Peter in bed at the end of the story

- To assemble the booklet: remove pages 44 through 50 from the children's books for them. Distribute paste and scissors. Supervise the children closely to see that they are cutting on the lines. First have them cut out the two pictures on page 44. Have them find page 49 and place the picture with the story title in the space where it belongs. Check responses before children paste.

- Next have children place the first picture, Rabbit family, in the first space on page 50. Point out that the shape of the picture matches the shape of the first space on page 50. Then have children cut out the first picture on page 46 and place it in the second space on page 50, matching shapes. Continue in this manner until all pictures are cut out and pasted in order.

- After the paste has dried, review the story "The Tale of Peter Rabbit" and have children point to each picture. Help the children fold the booklet on the dashed line. Read the words "The End" on the last page of the booklet.

LISTENING/SPEAKING SKILLS

Divide the class into small groups. Have children take turns telling each other the story of Peter Rabbit from the pictures in their booklets. Remind them to check each other to see that the story events are in the proper order.

HELPING ATYPICAL LEARNERS

Disabled: Have the tape of "Peter Rabbit" from Lesson 28 available for auditory learners. (*Tape Recorder,* A-1)

Spanish Speaking: Use the *Substitution* format to provide practice for using *he.* Give students a sentence that has a male subject noun. Students replace the noun with *he* and say the sentence. Change the pattern so that you use *he* in your sentence, and students replace it with a male subject noun. Use the same format to provide practice for using *she.*

ADDITIONAL ACTIVITIES

Easy: Have children take turns acting out the story "The Tale of Peter Rabbit" as you read the story aloud. Characters needed are: Mother Rabbit, Flopsy, Mopsy, Cottontail, Peter, Mr. McGregor, sparrows, the mouse, and the cat.

Challenging: Talk about other adventures Peter Rabbit might have. Ask students to use their imaginations. You might want to write the adventures they tell about on chart paper or have them draw pictures to illustrate the events.

Unit 3

OVERVIEW

The lessons in Unit 3 build upon the framework of skills established in the previous units. In this unit, children are working with a greater number of instructional concepts. They are learning to recognize the letters of the alphabet, both upper- and lower-case forms, and clue words for each letter. They talk about occupations that they might want to have in the future.

INTRODUCING THE UNIT

Bulletin Boards

- Since children will be learning to recognize letters in this unit, display an alphabet strip as a writing model and for children to practice associating letter names with letter forms. Begin by displaying pictures of objects whose names begin with the letters *a–g.* (Apple, ball, cat, dog, elephant, fish, and girl can easily be found in magazines.) Have the children take turns identifying each letter and the picture that accompanies it, saying a sentence such as "*a* is for *apple.*"

  After a few days change the bulletin board pictures to accompany the letters *h–n.* (Hat, ice, jet, kite, lock, man, nurse are suggestions.) Continue with *o–u* (orange, pan, quilt, ring, soap, tie, umbrella), and finally *v–z.* (van, watch, X-ray, yarn, zebra)

- Gather a collection of pictures to stimulate class discussion about real and make-believe. Divide the display into two parts. Label one part "Real." Mount pictures of real things such as an apartment building, school, factory, animals, books, cars, people eating, talking, and playing. Label the other part of the bulletin board "Make-Believe." Here show pictures of fantasies, such as characters from science-fiction, nursery rhymes, and make-believe stories like "Henny Penny" or "The Three Billy Goats Gruff."

  Ask children to take turns selecting a picture and talking about whether the things in the picture are real or make-believe. Ask how they can tell. Talk about how the stories we enjoy reading are sometimes about things that really happen and sometimes about make-believe happenings. Both kinds of stories can be enjoyable to read.

- Children will talk about careers during this unit. Focus on different occupations by creating a bulletin board titled "People Working." Display pictures of men, women, and children engaged in occupations familiar to children. (doctor, bus driver, construction worker, teacher, newspaper carrier, artist, and so on) Talk about the skills and talents each career requires. Encourage children to discuss which job they would like to have when they grow up and why.

Game: In Unit 3, children fine-tune their visual discrimination skills by recognizing similarities and differences in picture details. To practice these skills in another medium, play "Pick-a-Button." Place an assortment of buttons in a bag with a drawstring. Have children take turns choosing two buttons from the bag. Then have the child describe as many differences and similarities between the two buttons as he or she can find. (One button has four holes; one has two. One button is blue and the other is green; one is square and the other is round.) Encourage children to use complete sentences as they describe the buttons.

Letter from the Teacher: You may wish to distribute copies of *Letter 3 from the Teacher* (page TE 118) for children to take home at this time.

LISTENING/SPEAKING ACTIVITIES

The following activities for developing listening and speaking skills may accompany any lesson within the unit and may be done at any time during the unit. (*Note:* If activities are spread over several days or weeks, the selection or song should be reviewed each time.)

ACTIVITY 1

Objectives

to listen to and learn a song
to review letter names and letter forms

Procedure

Teach the "Alphabet Song", Resource Unit, page TE 109. Add hand or body movements as appropriate. (pointing to self, turning to left, reaching for the sky, and so on) Have children take turns pointing to letters on the alphabet strip or holding up alphabet cards as the song is sung. You may want to teach the song in several small segments, having children learn a phrase or small group of letters at a time.

ACTIVITY 2

Objectives

to listen to poems
to associate letter names with clue words

Procedure

At various times during the unit, read one of the poems by Phyllis McGinley, Resource Unit, page TE 109. Begin with the poem "*F* Is the Fighting Firetruck." Ask which words in the title begin with the letter *F*. Have children listen to the poem for what it tells about a firetruck. (color, siren, speed) Read the poem again. Ask children to listen for words that begin with *f*. (*fighting, firetruck, flaming, follows, fast, flies, furious, flashes*) Follow a similar procedure with the poem "*S* Is the Snorting Subway." (*snorting, subway, slithers, sort, scaly, sound, sometimes, stand, see, shivery*)

For the remaining poem, do not ask children to listen for vowel sounds. Merely point out that *e* is the first letter in the word *escalator*.

Talk about words in each poem that tell how things move. (*flash, slither, race, glide, scramble*) You might list the words on chart paper and read them aloud. Encourage children to use these words in sentences of their own.

Ask children why buses pull over to the curb when a firetruck approaches. (to get out of the way) Ask what cars should do. (pull over to the side also) Ask how you can "climb and climb and yet stand still." (on an escalator)

30 Capital Letters

OBJECTIVES
to recognize capital letters and their names

to associate letters with illustrated words

to place letters in alphabetical order

INSTRUCTIONAL VOCABULARY
capital letter   alphabet

ORAL VOCABULARY
United States   octopus

map

BASIC LESSON MATERIALS
scissors

LESSON STEPS

• Have children turn to page 51. Point out the letters of the alphabet. Explain that the letters on this page are all capital letters. Sing the ''Alphabet Song'' with the children. Tell children to point to each letter as they sing. Be sure to sing the song slowly so that the children have time to locate each letter.

• Ask children to find the first letter in their names and point to the letter.

Capital Letters

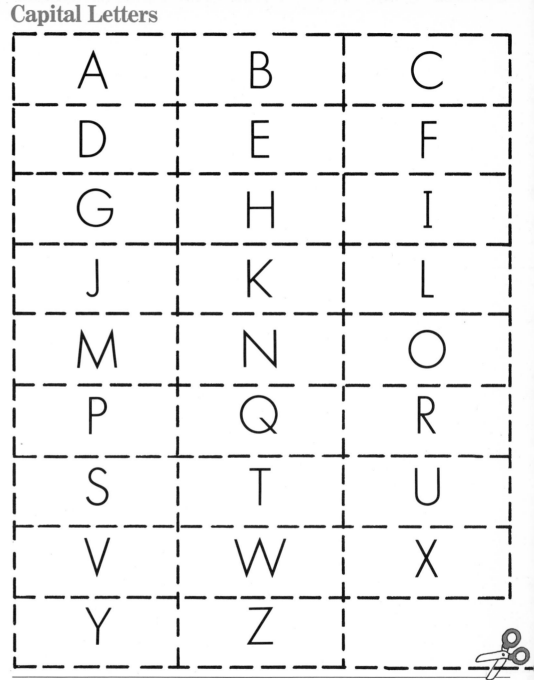

ACTIVITY: naming capital and small letters

OBJECTIVE: to identify capital and small letters

Capital Letters

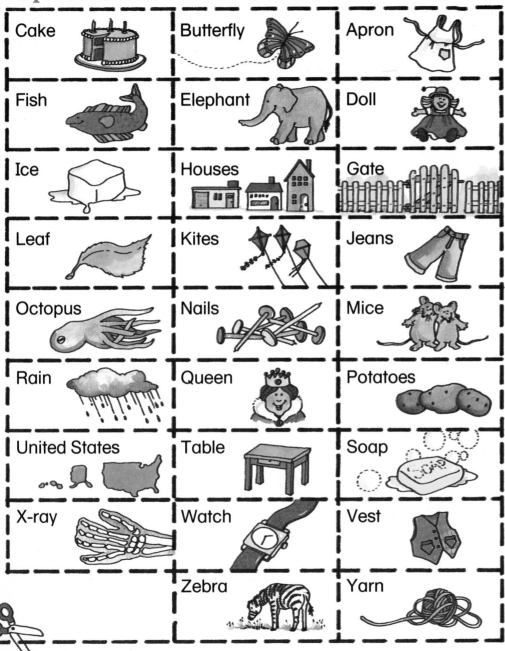

Cake	Butterfly	Apron
Fish	Elephant	Doll
Ice	Houses	Gate
Leaf	Kites	Jeans
Octopus	Nails	Mice
Rain	Queen	Potatoes
United States	Table	Soap
X-ray	Watch	Vest
	Zebra	Yarn

- Remind the children that letters stand for sounds. Explain that all the letters together make up the alphabet. Have children say the word *alphabet*.

- Distribute blunt scissors and remind the children to use them carefully. Have children cut out each rectangle on the page. Tell them that there is a picture on the other side of each letter to help them remember the letter name. Have children name each letter and help them identify the pictures on the reverse sides. Tell them that they now have their own alphabet card sets.

- Identify each picture with the children. Say: "*A* is for *Apron,*" and so on. Do not expect children to be able to read the words, but help them to understand that each word is pictured.

- If your classroom has an alphabet strip, have children put their alphabet letters in order on their desks, using the strip as a model.

- Give children envelopes in which to keep their alphabet card sets.

- Take time to review the alphabet as needed. Encourage children to practice with their alphabet letter sets on their own, naming the letters and using the pictures as clues.

This lesson is continued on the next page.

Lesson 30 (continued)

LISTENING/SPEAKING SKILLS

Ask small groups of children to recite the alphabet.

HELPING ATYPICAL LEARNERS

Disabled: For auditory learners to use for review and practice, record the class singing the "Alphabet Song." (*Tape Recorder,* A-1) Provide alphabet strips for students to paste on their alphabet envelopes.

ADDITIONAL ACTIVITIES

Easy: Have children work in pairs. Have them work with a set of capital letters. Children take turns identifying a letter; as each identifies a letter correctly, the child keeps the letter. The winner is the child who has the most letters. You might make the game more challenging by having the picture named, asking children to use the model sentences. ("*A* is for *Apron, B* is for *Bike,*" and so on)

Challenging: Have children fold a paper in four parts. Ask them to choose any four letters of the alphabet and, in each part of the paper, draw a picture whose name begins with the sound the letter stands for. Remind children to write the letter beside each picture.

OBJECTIVES

to recognize lower-case letters and their names

to associate letters with illustrated words

to place letters in alphabetical order

INSTRUCTIONAL VOCABULARY

small letter

ORAL VOCABULARY

fan   worm

igloo   valentine

owl

BASIC LESSON MATERIALS

scissors

LESSON STEPS

- Have children turn to page 53. Point out the letters of the alphabet. Explain that the letters on this page are all small letters. Sing the "Alphabet Song" with the children. Tell them to point to each letter as they sing. Be sure to sing the song slowly so that children have time to locate each letter as they sing.

- Distribute blunt scissors and remind children to use them carefully. Have children cut out the letters on the dashed lines.

- Help children name the picture on the back of each letter. Say the name of each letter and picture in this way: "a is for *apple*."

This lesson is continued on the next page.

Small Letters

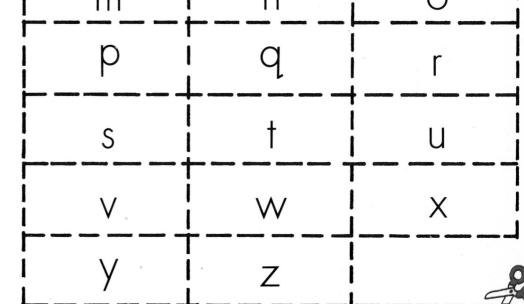

a	b	c
d	e	f
g	h	i
j	k	l
m	n	o
p	q	r
s	t	u
v	w	x
y	z	

TE 87

From Ginn English Program Grade K, copyrighted by Ginn and Company.   LIFE AND STUDY SKILLS: Naming Letters 53

Lesson 31 (continued)

- Give children envelopes in which to keep their alphabet card sets. Encourage them to practice with their alphabet sets on their own, naming the letters and using the pictures as clues.

LISTENING/SPEAKING SKILLS

Ask children to take turns naming letters that others point to at random.

HELPING ATYPICAL LEARNERS

Disabled: Provide alphabet strips for students to paste on their alphabet envelopes.

ADDITIONAL ACTIVITIES

Easy: Tape-record the class singing the alphabet song if possible. Have children listen to the tape and point to the letters as they are named. Then have children work in pairs and ask each other to name the letters as they point.

Challenging: Have children search in newspapers for letters that you designate. Ask them to draw a red circle around each example they find.

Small Letters

cats
bat
apple
fan
eggs
dog
igloo
hat
girl
lamp
keys
jacket
owls
nest
mittens
rabbit
quilt
pencils
umbrella
top
sandwich
x-ray
worms
valentine
zipper
yard

32 Alike and Different

OBJECTIVES
to visually discriminate picture detail

to recognize variations in two details

to recognize differences in pictured items

ORAL VOCABULARY
tire swing   factory

BASIC LESSON MATERIALS
none

LESSON STEPS

- Have children turn to page 55. Ask them to find row 1 and help them to identify the first picture in the row. (bicycle) Ask: "Do all the pictures in row 1 look the same as the first one?" (No, one is different.) Have the children point to the picture that looks different, and tell why. (It is missing a front wheel.) Tell children to mark an *X* on the picture that looks different. Identify each picture with the children as they work on the page.

- Follow a similar procedure for each row. Tell children to find and mark an *X* on the picture in each row that looks different from the first picture. In each row, ask children why the picture looks different. (*row* 2—no tire; *row* 3—no door; *row* 4—hand is open)

This lesson is continued on the next page.

Alike and Different

1.

2.

3.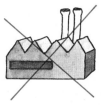

4.

ACTIVITY: marking an *X* on pictures that look different from the first pictures in the rows

OBJECTIVE: to recognize pictures that are alike and different

TE 89

HELPING ATYPICAL LEARNERS

Nonstandard English: Speakers of nonstandard English may need help with comparatives. ("This one is more different.") Model the standard usage for children to hear and practice.

ADDITIONAL ACTIVITIES

Easy: Have children work in pairs or small groups. Tell them to find three classroom items (books, blocks, math rods, manipulatives), two the same and one different. Tell the children to assemble the items and show them to another group of children. Have the other group find the item that is different. Encourage children to make the activity challenging by choosing an item that is not drastically different. Encourage children to tell why the item is different.

Challenging: Have children draw four circles or four squares. Tell them to decorate each shape with the same design, but on one shape add or leave out one design detail. You might want to illustrate an example on the chalkboard. Say: "Make one design a little different from the rest." Have children show their designs to the class and ask the rest of the children to find the design that is different. Encourage children to tell why it is different.

Real and Make-Believe

OBJECTIVES

to distinguish reality from fantasy

to recognize variations in three details

to visually discriminate picture detail

ORAL VOCABULARY

gym	groceries
tennis racket	clerk
pompom	checkout counter
fruit	wand
vegetable	

BASIC LESSON MATERIALS

paste   scissors

LESSON STEPS

Note: After students complete the work on text page 57 and have removed cutouts page 58, the real supermarket on page 56 and the make-believe supermarket on page 59 will be opposite each other in their texts.

• Explain that children will do page 56 at a later time. Tell them to turn to page 57. Say: "This time you will have to look very carefully to find the one picture in each row that looks different."

This lesson is continued on the next four pages.

Real and Make-Believe

ACTIVITY: placing pictures of real objects in a scene   OBJECTIVE: to distinguish between real and make-believe

Lesson 33 (continued)

- Talk about the first picture in row 1. Ask children to describe what they see. (boy in long pants and long-sleeved shirt, hands on hips) Have children point to a picture that looks the same as the first picture. Ask: "Which picture does not look exactly the same?" (picture 4) "How does it look different?" (boy is wearing shorts) Have the children mark an *X* on the last picture.

- Follow a similar procedure for each row. Tell children to find and mark an *X* on the picture in each row that looks different from the first picture. In each row ask why the picture looks different. (*row 2*—no tennis racket; *row 3*—no pompons; *row 4*—no spoon)

- Although this lesson continues with cutting and pasting activities involving text pages 56, 58, and 59, you may wish to break it at this point, completing the remainder in another session.

- Should you wish to complete the lesson in one session, continue with the Lesson-Steps on page TE 93.

LISTENING/SPEAKING SKILLS

Ask two children who are dressed similarly (shirt and pants; blouse and skirt; similar sweaters or belts) to stand. Ask children to talk about how their clothes are alike (color, style, decorative design) and how they are different. Encourage the use of complete sentences as children talk about likenesses and differences.

TE 92

Alike and Different

1.

2.

3.

4.

ACTIVITY: marking an *X* on pictures that look different from the first pictures in the rows

OBJECTIVE: to recognize pictures that are alike and different

VISUAL SKILLS: Telling Alike and Different **57**

Real and Make-Believe

Child will place the real objects on page 56 and the make-believe objects on page 59.

ACTIVITY: placing pictures of make-believe objects in a scene

OBJECTIVE: to distinguish between real and make-believe

LESSON STEPS

- Next have children look at the pictures on page 58. Explain that there are two kinds of pictures on the page—real and make-believe. Ask: "Who can find a picture of something that looks real?" (family with shopping cart; fruits and vegetables; girl holding two shopping bags; clerk at checkout counter) Ask where the children might see people or things like those in the picture. (at a supermarket)

- Talk about the make-believe pictures. Ask: "Who can find a picture of something that looks make-believe?" (elf pushing shopping cart; dragon buying cereal; vegetables with arms and legs; a hen holding loaves of bread) "Would you really see things like these in the picture?" (no)

- Have the children look at page 56. Ask: "What do you see?" (a supermarket) "Does this look real or make-believe?" (real) "Which people or things from page 58 would you see in the real supermarket?"

TE 93

Lesson 33 (continued)

- Have children turn to page 59. Ask: "What kind of store do you see on this page?" (make-believe) "How do you know?" (rabbit as checkout clerk; bucket, brooms, cans, and boxes with faces; grocery items with legs and arms) "Would you really see things like those in the picture?" (no)

- Distribute blunt scissors and paste. Remind children to use scissors and paste carefully. Have children cut out the pictures of real things from page 58 and paste them onto page 56. (family with cart, fruits and vegetables, girl with shopping bags clerk at checkout counter) Then have children cut out the pictures of make-believe things from page 58 and paste them onto page 59. (elf, dragon, vegetables with legs, hen with bread)

LISTENING/SPEAKING SKILLS

Have children talk about stories they could make up using the completed pictures on pages 56 and 59. You might suggest that they give names to the people in the picture of the real supermarket and tell what they might have bought in the supermarket. Encourage children to dictate make-believe events using the picture of the make-believe store.

TE 94

HELPING ATYPICAL LEARNERS

Nonstandard English: Provide a model of the standard usage of the verb *see* if children use the nonstandard version. ("I seen a book.")

ADDITIONAL ACTIVITIES

Easy: Ask children to fold drawing paper in half. On one side have them draw something that is real. You might suggest an animal or food or a person. On the other side have them draw something make-believe. You might suggest a horse with wings; a dog with a wig, a person with wheels. After the drawings are completed, display them and have children describe their drawings. Encourage others to tell why the make-believe picture is not real.

Challenging: Assemble a group of picture books from your classroom library or from the school library. Have children divide the books into two categories, one of stories that could really happen, and one of make-believe stories.

OBJECTIVES

to recognize variations in four details

to visually discriminate picture detail

to recognize the differences in pictured items

ORAL VOCABULARY

helmet   uniform
elbow pads   safety
knee pads

BASIC LESSON MATERIALS

LESSON STEPS

• Have children look at the pictures on page 60. Ask them what they think they will be doing on this page. (finding pictures that are different)

• For each row, say: "Tell me about the first picture in the row." Identify the details of the pictures with the children. Say: "Now look at the other pictures in the row. Can you find the one that is not the same as the first picture? How is it different? Mark an *X* on the picture that is different." Encourage children to answer in complete sentences.

row 1—girl in gym outfit with roller skates, helmet, elbow pads, knee pads; picture 3 is different—no helmet.

row 2—boy in baseball uniform, with bat on shoulder; picture 2 is different—no bat

row 3—girl with skates, helmet, and knee pads; picture 4 is different—no knee pads

row 4—boy with uniform and bat; picture 4 is different—no helmet

LISTENING/SPEAKING SKILLS

Talk about safety when playing games in which children may fall or be hurt. Ask children to look at the picture of the girl on roller skates on page 60. Talk about her safety equipment. Ask why she has a helmet and knee pads. (to protect her head and knees) Ask: "What do people who play baseball wear for safety?" (helmet, pads, gloves, or mitts) "Can you think of what people wear in a car or plane for safety?" (safety belts) "What about workers who build houses or bridges?" (hard hats) "Cooks?" (pot holders) "Football players?" (helmets, pads)

ADDITIONAL ACTIVITIES

Easy: Draw three simple flowers on the chalkboard. Put two leaves on the stems of two flowers and one leaf on the stem of a third. Draw three stick figures, two with hair and a third with no hair. Draw three triangles, two with lines inside the triangle slanting in one direction and one with lines slanting in another direction. Ask children to find the picture that looks different and mark an *X* on it.

Challenging: Write the following groups of letter strings in three rows on the chalkboard:

tsp	tsp	pst
opm	mpo	opm
bed	deb	bed

Help children name the letters in each letter string as you point from left to right. Point to the first letter string in the row. Ask which letter string is the same as the first letter string on the left, and which is different. Have children mark an *X* on the letter string that is different.

ACTIVITY: marking an *X* on pictures that look different from the first pictures in the rows

OBJECTIVE: to recognize pictures that are alike and different

OBJECTIVES
to identify workers, their jobs and tools

to discuss occupations

to discuss the abilities, talents, and skills needed for certain jobs

ORAL VOCABULARY
eye doctor   carpenter

plumber

BASIC LESSON MATERIALS
none

LESSON STEPS

• Talk about the many jobs people do. Ask children to talk about jobs held by people they know or have heard about. Explain that people do different kinds of work.

• Have the children look at the pictures on page 61. Say: "Look at the first picture in row 1. What do you see?" (an eye doctor and a patient) You might explain that the real name of an eye doctor is *ophthalmologist*. "Now look at the picture next to it. What do you think has happened?" (The patient has eye glasses.) Talk about what an eye doctor does. (examines people's eyes to keep them healthy; recommends glasses if they are needed; sends the person to someone who will make the glasses)

• Talk about other types of workers who help keep people healthy or take care of them when they are sick. (nurses, dentists, family doctors)

• Ask children to look at the pictures in row 2. Ask "Who do you see in the first picture?" (plumber) "Now what do you see in the picture next to the plumber?" (leaking faucet) "Why is the picture of the leaking faucet next to the picture of a plumber?" Talk about what a plumber does. (puts in water pipes, fixes leaks or breaks in pipes, unclogs drains)

• Ask children to look at the pictures in row 3. Ask: "Who do you see in the first picture?" (carpenter) "What does a carpenter do?" (makes things from wood) Talk about the picture next to the carpenter. (unfinished house) Ask what the carpenter will need to do to finish the house. (roof, doors, windows, steps)

• Ask the children to look at the pictures in row 4. Ask: "Who do you see in the first picture?" (truck driver) "What is happening in the picture next to the truck driver?" (The driver is delivering something.)

LISTENING/SPEAKING SKILLS

Have children dictate a list of jobs they might like to have when they grow up. If they have difficulty, you might add some suggestions. (baker, store clerk, engineer, pilot, dancer, scientist) Encourage children to tell why they would choose any of these jobs. Remind them to speak in complete sentences.

HELPING ATYPICAL LEARNERS

Disabled: Focus children's thoughts on the pictures by asking Yes-No questions. (*Yes-No Questions,* D-1) When students offer information about the pictures, they should speak in complete sentences.

Nonstandard English: As children talk about jobs, watch for nonstandard uses of the verbs *is* and *see.* ("She be a doctor." "I seen the plumber.") Model standard usage of the verbs for oral practice.

ADDITIONAL ACTIVITIES

Easy: Explain that pictures can tell a whole story. Display several picture books from the school library. Talk about what words children might use to tell the stories in these books. Then have children take turns "reading" stories to the class, using the pictures as they tell the stories.

Challenging: Have children work in pairs and choose a job to pantomime for the class to guess. You might suggest some jobs if children need ideas. (doctor, dentist, fire fighter, artist, carpenter, truck driver)

Jobs

ACTIVITY: talking about workers and their tools

OBJECTIVE: to identify workers, their jobs, and tools

LIFE AND STUDY SKILLS: Naming People Who Help **61**

OBJECTIVES
to create original art
to project oneself into the future
to talk about an occupation

INSTRUCTIONAL VOCABULARY
sentence

ORAL VOCABULARY
frame

BASIC LESSON MATERIALS
crayons

LESSON STEPS

- Point to the picture frame on page 62. Read the word *me* at the top of the frame. Remind children that at the beginning of this book they made pictures of themselves in a frame like this one. If children have not removed page 1, have them turn back to see the pictures they made.

- Tell children that the pictures they will make on this page will show what they may look like when they grow up. Talk about some of the jobs children discussed in Lesson 35. (doctor, plumber, carpenter, truck driver) Add other jobs to the list. (lawyer, pilot, nurse, clerk, factory worker, teacher, mail carrier, computer programmer, writer, farmer, homemaker, bus driver, artist, cook, animal trainer, engineer, musician, weather predictor, scientist) Say: "Decide what job you would like most to have when you grow up. Imagine how you would look doing that job. In the frame on page 62, draw yourself doing the job you would like."

LISTENING/SPEAKING SKILLS

Have children take turns showing the pictures they drew. Ask them to tell the class about their pictures.

HELPING ATYPICAL LEARNERS

Spanish Speaking: Use the *Substitution* format to provide practice with past and present tenses. Give a sentence in the present tense, and students respond with the sentence in the past tense. Continue the practice by giving sentences in the past and requiring a change to the present.

ADDITIONAL ACTIVITIES

Easy: Give children sentence starters such as "If I were a dancer, I would. . . ." Have them complete the sentences. ("I would be on television.") Some suggestions might be:

"If I were a scientist. . . ."
"If I were a writer. . . ."
"If I were a pilot. . . ."

Challenging: Ask children who like to tell stories to select a picture from a magazine and make up a story about it. Children may work in small groups and add to each others' stories. Then have the groups share their stories with the class. You might write their stories on chart paper and read them aloud.

HANDWRITING ACTIVITY

Say: "Look carefully at the words on the bottom of page 62. Do you remember where you saw them before?" (at the end of the little book made about "The Tale of Peter Rabbit") "Who can remember what these words are?" *(The End)* "Why do you think the words are here?" (This is the end of the book.) Have children trace and write the words *The End*.

Telling about Me

Child will draw herself or himself grown up and employed here.

ME

The End

ACTIVITY: drawing a self-portrait   OBJECTIVE: to picture oneself in a future occupation

TE 101
ABCDEFGHIJ0898765
Printed in the United States of America

Resource Unit

For use with Unit 1, page TE 4

MORNING GREETING

Ena B. Knippel

Brightly

We come to school to work and play, Good morn - ing! Good morn - ing!
Good after - noon! Good after - noon!

It's such a {bright and sun - ny day,} Good morn - ing! Good morn - ing!
{wet and rain - y day,} Good after - noon! Good after - noon!
{gray and cloud - y day,}

For use with Unit 1, Lesson 3, pages TE 9–11

MARY HAD A LITTLE LAMB

Mary had a little lamb,
Its fleece was white as snow;
And everywhere that Mary went
The lamb was sure to go.

It followed her to school one day,
That was against the rule;
It made the children laugh and play
To see a lamb at school.

And so the teacher turned it out,
But still it lingered near;
And waited patiently about
Till Mary did appear.

"Why does the lamb love Mary so?"
The eager children cry;
"Why, Mary loves the lamb, you know,"
The teacher did reply.

—*Sarah Josepha Hale*

For use with Unit 1, page TE 4

TIPTOE

Yesterday I skipped all day,
The day before I ran,
Today I'm going to tiptoe
Everywhere I can.
I'll tiptoe down the stairway.
I'll tiptoe through the door.
I'll tiptoe to the living room
And give an awful roar
And my father, who is reading,
Will jump up from his chair
And mumble something silly like
"I didn't see you there."
I'll tiptoe to my mother
And give a little cough
And when she spins to see me
Why, I'll softly tiptoe off.
I'll tiptoe through the meadows,
Over hills and yellow sands
And when my toes get tired
Then I'll tiptoe on my hands.

—*Karla Kuskin*

For use with Unit 1, Lesson 2, pages TE 7–TE 8

A LITTLE BOY WENT WALKING

Emilie Poulsson

Cornelia C. Roeske

Moderately

1. A lit-tle boy went walk-ing One love-ly sum-mer's day.

He met a lit-tle rab-bit That quick-ly hopped a-way.

2. He saw a shining river
Go winding in and out,
And little fishes in it
Were swimming all about.

4. The bridge above the water
Was where he stopped to rest,
And there along the bank was
A little sparrow's nest.

3. And as he watched the birdies
Above the treetops fly,
He saw the clouds go sailing
Across the sunny sky.

5. He saw the big church steeple,
The flow'rs that summer brings.
He said, "I'll go tell Mother
I've seen so many things."

For use with Unit 1, Lesson 3, pages TE 9–11

OLD KING COLE

Old King Cole
Was a merry old soul,
And a merry old soul was he;
He called for his pipe,
And he called for his bowl,
And he called for his fiddlers three.

Every fiddler, he had a fiddle,
And a very fine fiddle had he;
Twee tweedle dee, tweedle dee, went the
fiddlers three.
Oh, there's none so rare
As can compare
With King Cole and his fiddlers three.

HUMPTY DUMPTY

Humpty Dumpty sat on a wall,
Humpty Dumpty had a great fall.
   All the king's horses,
   And all the king's men,
Couldn't put Humpty together again.

LITTLE MISS MUFFET

Little Miss Muffet
Sat on a tuffet,
Eating her curds and whey;
There came a big spider,
Who sat down beside her
And frightened Miss Muffet away.

Resource Unit

For use with Unit 1, Lesson 9, pages TE 25–27

LITTLE DUCKLING TRIES HIS VOICE

Once upon a time a fat Little Duckling went on a journey into the wide world. He wandered along the barnyard road, and presently he saw a Kitty Cat.

"Me-ow!" said the Kitty Cat.

"O-o-oh!" cried the Little Duckling. "Isn't that a pretty sound! I think I'll talk that way!"

But do you suppose the Little Duckling could say "Me-ow"?

No, indeed!

He tried, but the best he could do was:

"Me-e-ack! Me-e-ack!"

And that wasn't pretty at all!

So the Little Duckling waddled on and on, and after a while he saw a Puppy Dog.

"Bow-wow!" said the Puppy Dog.

"O-o-oh!" cried the Little Duckling. "Isn't that a lovely noise! I think I'll talk that way!"

But do you suppose the Little Duckling could say "Bow-wow"?

No, indeed!

He tried, but this is the way he sounded:

"B—ack! B—ack!"

And that wasn't lovely at all!

Then the Little Duckling waddled on and on, and soon he saw a Yellow Bird in a tree.

"Tweet—tweet tweet—tweet tweet!" sang the Yellow Bird.

"O-o-oh!" signed the Little Duckling softly. "Isn't that a sweet song! I think I'll sing that way!"

But do you suppose the Little Duckling could sing "Tweet—tweet"?

No, indeed!

He tried his very best, but all he could say was:

"Tw—ack! Tw-ack!"

And that wasn't sweet at all!

So the Little Duckling waddled on and on, and after a time he saw a Big Cow.

"Moo-o-o!" said the Big Cow.

"O-o-oh!" thought the Little Duckling. "Isn't that a bea-u-tiful roar! I think I'll roar that way!"

But do you suppose the Little Duckling could say "Moo-o-o"?

No, indeed!

He tried, but all he could manage was:

"M—ack! M—ack!"

And that wasn't bea-u-tiful at all!

The Little Duckling was very sad.

He could not say "Me-ow" like the Kitty Cat.

He could not say "Bow-wow" like the Puppy Dog.

He could not say "Tweet-tweet" like the Yellow Bird.

He could not say "Moo-o-o" like the Big Cow.

He waddled slowly on and on. All at once he saw his own Mother Duck coming toward him along the barnyard road.

"Quack! Quack!" cried Mother Duck.

"O-o-oh!" whispered the Little Duckling happily to himself. "That's the prettiest sound in the whole wide world! I think I'll talk that way!"

And he found that he could say, "Quack! Quack!" very nicely.

—*Marjorie M. La Fleur*

For use with Unit 2, page TE 37

CURIOSITY

Tell me, tell me everything!
  What makes it Winter
  And then Spring?
  Which are the children
  Butterflies?
  Why do people keep
  Winking their eyes?
  Where do birds sleep?
  Do bees like to sting?
Tell me, tell me please, everything!

Tell me, tell me, I want to know!
  What makes leaves grow
  In the shapes they grow?
  Why do goldfish
  Keep chewing? and rabbits
  Warble their noses?
  Just from habits?
  Where does the wind
  When it goes away go?
Tell me! or don't even grown-ups know?

—*Harry Behn*

For use with Unit 2, Lesson 14, pages TE 38–TE 39

LITTLE RED RIDING HOOD

A long time ago in a great wood far away, there lived a little girl who was much loved by her mother and her grandmother. The grandmother had a little coat and hood of red velvet made for her granddaughter. The little girl looked so pretty in it that her friends for miles around began to call her Little Red Riding Hood.

One day Little Red Riding Hood's mother baked a cake and made fresh butter. She said to Little Red Riding Hood, "Go, my dear, and take this cake and a pot of fresh butter to your grandmother. She is not well, I hear, and you will find her resting in bed."

Little Red Riding Hood loved her grandmother and wanted to help her. So she put the things in a basket and set out at once for the cottage on the other side of the wood where her grandmother lived.

Just as she came to the edge of the wood, Red Riding Hood met a wolf who said to her, "Good morning, Little Red Riding Hood."

"Good morning, Master Wolf," replied the little girl, who had no thought of being afraid, for all the animals of the wood were her friends.

"Where are you going, Little Red Riding Hood?" asked the wolf.

"I am going to visit my grandmother," replied Little Red Riding Hood. "I am taking her a cake and a pot of butter, for she is ill."

"And where does your grandmother live?" asked the wolf.

"Down past the mill, on the other side of the wood," said Little Red Riding Hood.

"Well, I don't mind if I go and see her, too," said the wolf. "I'll take this road, and you take that, and we shall see which of us will be there first."

He knew well enough that he had chosen the nearest way. He would dash through the underbrush, swim a pond, and by a very short cut, bring himself to the grandmother's door. He guessed, too, that the little girl would stop to pick strawberries in the wood and gather a bouquet of wild flowers for her grandmother.

And sure enough, the wolf who cared neither for strawberries nor wild flowers, was very soon at the cottage. He had stopped only long enough to eat some honey so that his voice would sound sweeter as he talked with Grandmother.

He knocked at the door with his paw, thump! thump!

"Who is there?" cried Grandmother.

"It is I, Little Red Riding Hood. I have come to see how you are, and to bring you a cake and a pot of butter," said the wolf, as well as he could. He tried to make his voice sound as sweet as that of the little girl.

"Please open the door and come in," called Grandmother from her bed.

The wolf opened the door, and in he went. When Grandmother saw him, she became so frightened she jumped out of bed and ran out the door as fast as she could go.

The wolf shut the door and got into the grandmother's bed, but first he put on her cap and nightgown. He laughed to think of the trick he was about to play on Little Red Riding Hood, who must soon be coming.

All this time, Red Riding Hood was picking strawberries and gathering wild flowers on her way through the wood.

By and by she came to her grandmother's cottage and gave a little tap at the door.

"Who is there?" cried the wolf.

The hoarse voice frightened Little Red Riding Hood, but she said to herself, "Poor Grandmother must have a bad cold."

"It is I, your Little Red Riding Hood," she said. "I have come to see how you are and to bring you a pot of butter and a cake from Mother."

"Open the door and come in," called the wolf. Little Red Riding Hood did so, and went into the cottage.

"Put the cake and butter on the table," said the wolf. "Then come and help me to rise." He had turned his face away so that Red Riding Hood saw only her grandmother's white cap.

Little Red Riding Hood put the basket of goodies on the table and went to the bed to do as she had been bidden. "Why Grandmother," she said, "what long arms you have!"

"The better to hug you with my dear," said the wolf.

"And, Grandmother, what long ears you have!"

"The better to hear you with, my dear."

"But, Grandmother, what big teeth you have!"

"The better to eat you with, my dear!" said the wolf. And he was just going to spring upon poor Little Red Riding Hood when a wasp flew into the room and stung him on the nose.

The wolf gave a cry and jumped out of Grandmother's bed. He was so frightened that he ran out the door and into the wood, never to be heard from again.

Soon Grandmother and a woodsman came hurrying toward the cottage from the wood.

(continued on next page)

Resource Unit

LITTLE RED RIDING HOOD (continued)

Little Red Riding Hood was overjoyed and ran to greet them. Then all three went into the cottage and sat down to enjoy the strawberries, the cake, and the butter which Little Red Riding Hood had brought.

—*Adapted from The Story of "Little Red Riding Hood" by Marion Florence Lansing*

For use with Unit 2, Lesson 21, pages TE 55–TE 57

SKIP AND WADDLE

Skip was a new baby chick, just out of his eggshell. He was yellow and soft and fluffy. He said "peep-peep" in a very squeaky voice.

Waddle was a new baby duck, just out of his eggshell. He was yellow and soft and fluffy. And he said "peep-peep" in a very squeaky voice.

When Skip and Waddle first looked at each other, they thought they were exactly alike. And they were—*almost.*

At night, Skip and Waddle slept together in a warm little box. During the day, they played together in a big outdoor pen. There was water to drink in a round pan. There was food to eat in a long pan. There was grass to nibble and soft dirt to scratch. There was a shady place to play and a sunshiny place to play.

Skip and Waddle were very happy friends until—THE DAY THEY FOUND OUT. On this particular morning, Skip and Waddle tumbled from their bed and hurried over to the long pan. Skip pecked at the food with his little pointed beak. Waddle scooped up the food with his long flat bill.

Skip peeped,
"Don't scoop, scoop, scoop,
And push the food around.
Just peck, peck, peck,
And keep it off the ground."
And he hopped into the food pan and scratched the food about with his feet.
"You scratch and scatter,
And that's no better,"
peeped Waddle as he waddled over to the round pan to scoop a big drink.

Skip hurried after Waddle. He didn't want to be left behind. He got to the water pan just in time to sip only a very little water, but no sooner had he dipped his pointed beak into the water than KERSPLASH! Waddle scrambled into the water, flapping his tiny wings furiously.
"Oh, me! Oh, my!
That's not the way to fly!"
peeped Skip.
"I'm swimming, silly Skip!
Come on in and take a dip,"
peeped Waddle.

But Skip hopped over to a patch of soft dirt and began to scratch for bugs and worms.

Waddle swam alone and Skip scratched alone until most of THE DAY was gone. Both friends were lonesome. But neither Skip nor Waddle left his favorite game until Skip found some sunflower seeds. Waddle loved sunflower seeds. He scrambled quickly out of the water and waddled over to the soft dirt where Skip was scratching. He hurried to scoop up every seed. Skip was so pleased with himself that he started to give Waddle a scratching lesson.

"Put your right foot out.
Poke your right toe in.
Bring your right foot back.
With your left begin.
Put your left foot out.
Poke your left toe in.
Bring your left foot back.
With your right begin."
Waddle tried to scratch, but he just couldn't do it. His toes would not turn in. His feet sprawled far apart. In fact, he fell right over backwards onto his stubby tail. KERPLUNK! He looked so funny that Skip laughed and laughed.

Waddle got up, wiggled the dust out of his tail, and peeped, "I tried your game, now you try mine."

Away they both raced to the water pan. But Skip didn't wait for Waddle to give him a swimming lesson. He jumped right into the water. Too bad! He sank right down to the bottom of the pan. Only by hopping on tiptoe could Skip keep his head out of the water until Waddle helped him out.

Skip was a very wet little chick. He snuggled down in a warm sunny place to dry out. Waddle went with him. The two friends were very quiet for a long time.

Suddenly Skip cried to Waddle,
    "Look down your nose!
    There's something thin
    Between your toes!
    It looks like skin."
Waddle held up one foot, then the other.
    "My webs! Indeed!
    They help me swim.
    That's what you need—
    Your toes are slim."
Skip held up one foot, then the other. His toes were long and slim, without any webs at all. His feet were different from Waddle's.

Then Waddle cried,
    "Your mouth is just a tip—
    That's why you peck and sip."
Skip answered,
    "Your mouth is long and flat,
    And so you scoop like that."
The two friends peeped together as they slipped into the warm little box and went to sleep,
    "Well, now we know! Now we know!
    There must be a difference
    In the way we grow."

After that Skip and Waddle spent their days together and apart. They always ate breakfast together. Then Waddle swam alone and Skip scratched alone. But they still sat in the sunshine or shade to talk, and at night they slept together in the warm box.

And they grew up. Waddle's legs stayed short and thick. Skip's legs grew long and thin. Skip's tail grew long and Waddle's tail stayed short. Both lost their soft yellow fluffiness. They grew feathers. Waddle's feathers were white and Skip's were red and brown. And Skip grew a little red comb on the top of his head.

Then one day a big black dog ran barking past their pen. He ran so fast and barked so loud that he frightened Skip and Waddle.

Waddle opened his mouth. "Quack-quack!" he said.

Skip opened his mouth. "Cock-a-doodle-doo!" he called.

The big black dog was soon gone and the two friends looked at each other in surprise.
    "Quack-quack-quack,"
said Waddle again as he looked at Skip.
    "Cock-a-doodle-doo,"
called Skip again as he looked at Waddle.
    "Now we know. Now we know.
    There is a difference
    In the way we grow."

—*Rose Cary O'Brian*

For use with Unit 2, Lesson 24, pages TE 62–TE 64

THE ELF AND THE DORMOUSE

1. Under a toadstool
    Crept a wee Elf,
Out of the rain
    To shelter himself.

    Under the toadstool,
    Sound asleep
    Sat a big Dormouse
    All in a heap.

2. Trembled the wee Elf,
    Frightened, and yet
Fearing to fly away
    Lest he get wet.

3. To the next shelter—
    Maybe a mile!
Suddenly the wee Elf
    Smiled a wee smile,

4. Tugged till the toadstool
    Toppled in two.
Holding it over him
    Gaily he flew.

5. Soon he was safe home
    Dry as could be.
6. Soon woke the Dormouse—
    "Good gracious me!

Where is my toadstool?"
    Loudly he lamented.
7. —And that's how umbrellas,
    First were invented.

—*Oliver Herford*

For use with Unit 2, Lesson 28, pages TE 74–TE 77

THE TALE OF PETER RABBIT

This is the story of Peter Rabbit.

"My dears," said Mrs. Rabbit one morning, "you may go into the fields or down the lane, but don't go into Mr. McGregor's garden. Your father had an accident there. Mr. and Mrs. McGregor made him into a rabbit stew. I am going shopping now, so run along and don't get into mischief."

Then Mrs. Rabbit took a basket and her umbrella and went through the wood to the baker's to buy a loaf of brown bread and five rolls. Flopsy, Mopsy, and Cottontail, who were good little rabbits, decided to go hopping down the lane to look for blackberries.

But Peter, who was naughty, disobeyed his mother. He ran away, straight to Mr. McGregor's garden, and squeezed under the gate. Peter had never seen so many nice vegetables! He ate and ate and ate and ate.

When Peter began to feel sick he went to look for some parsley, because he had heard that parsley was good rabbit medicine. He came around a cucumber vine and whom should he meet but Mr. McGregor himself!

Mr. McGregor was down on his hands and knees planting cabbages. When he saw Peter, he jumped up and picked up his rake. Then he ran after Peter, shouting angrily: "Stop, thief!"

Peter was dreadfully frightened; he rushed here and there, all around the garden, for he had forgotten the way back to the gate. He lost one shoe in the cabbages and the other shoe in the beans.

He kept running faster and faster and just then he got caught in a gooseberry bush. He was wearing his new blue jacket with the large brass buttons. The buttons got caught in the bushes and held him tight.

Peter gave himself up for lost and started to cry, but the sparrows, who were watching, flew down and said, "You must try hard to get free. Run, Peter, run!"

So Peter tried hard and got free, but he slipped out of his nice new jacket which was caught in the gooseberry bush.

He ran into the tool shed and jumped into a sprinkling can. It would have been a fine place to hide if it had not had so much water in it.

Mr. McGregor came looking for him in the shed. Just then Peter sneezed. He heard Mr. McGregor coming, so he jumped out of the window, upsetting three pots of flowers. He ran as fast as he could but still he could not find the gate.

An old mouse came running by carrying peas and beans home to her family in the wood. Peter asked her the way to the gate but she could not talk with such a big bean in her mouth—or maybe she was too polite to talk with her mouth full. She just nodded her head. Peter began to cry.

Just then he saw a big old white cat. She was swishing her tail. Peter had heard about cats, so he did not dare to stop to talk with her to ask which way to go. He went the other way!

Suddenly, he heard the noise of a hoe—scr-r-ritch, scratch, scratch, scritch. When Peter looked up he saw Mr. McGregor hoeing his onions. His back was turned toward Peter and beyond him was the gate.

Peter made up his mind to run as fast as he could.

He squeezed under the gate and never stopped running until he got home, under the root of the big fir tree.

He was so tired he lay down and closed his eyes. Then he remembered how sick he was.

Mother Rabbit was busy cooking dinner, but she wondered where Peter had lost his shoes and nice blue jacket. That was the second jacket, and the second pair of shoes he had lost in a week. What a naughty boy!

Peter had eaten too many green vegetables and he felt terrible. He was so sick that his mother gave him a big dose of medicine and put him to bed. Bad little Peter Rabbit!

But Flopsy, Mopsy, and Cottontail, who were good little rabbits, had blackberries, sugar, and cream.

—*Adapted from Beatrix Potter's Story by L. E. Watters*

For use with Unit 3, page TE 83

ALPHABET SONG
Levin Houston

A - B - C, Now take a look at me, D - E - F, I'm turn-ing to the left, G - H - I, I'm reach-ing for the sky, J - K - L, (and) M - N - O, just try it fast, or try it slow; P - Q - R, and S - T - U, Now I'm do-ing some-thing new, V - W - X, Now what comes next? Let me see_ Y and Z, the alpha-bet's eas-y as A - B - C! A - B - C, D - E - F, G - H - I, J - K - L, M - N - O - P - Q - R, S - T - U, V - W - X, Y and Z, the alpha- bet's eas- y as A - B - C, Hoo- ray for me!

For use with Unit 3, page TE 83

Three poems by Phyllis McGinley

F IS THE FIGHTING FIRETRUCK

F is the fighting Firetruck
   That's painted a flaming red.
When the signals blast
It follows fast
   While the chief flies on ahead.
And buses pull to the curbing
   At the siren's furious cry,
For early or late,
They have to wait
   When the Firetruck flashes by.

S IS THE SNORTING SUBWAY

S is the snorting Subway
   That slithers below the ground.
It's sort of a scaly dragon.
   It roars with a dragon sound.
And sometimes far
In the foremost car
   The motorman lets you stand
To see the place
Where the dragons race
   Through their dark and shivery land.

E IS THE ESCALATOR

E is the Escalator
   That gives an elegant ride.
You step on the stair
With an easy air
   And up and up you glide.
It's nicer than scaling ladders
   Or scrambling 'round a hill,
For you climb and climb
But all the time
   You're really standing still.

Helping Atypical Learners

Differing ability levels and backgrounds are expected in the classroom population. Throughout this Teacher's Edition, the "Helping Atypical Learners" sections provide useful activities written by experts for disabled learners, Spanish-speaking learners, and speakers of nonstandard English.

Any student's learning style is a composite of traits. One student may have excellent skills in grammar, for example, but poor skills in written or oral expression. Students also learn in different ways at different times.

You will find, therefore, that many of the activities suggested for atypical learners may also be applied for whole-class use. Indeed, some may already be part of your normal classroom procedure. If teacher aides are available to you, they may be assigned to prepare such materials as tape recordings and manipulatives and to participate in the one-to-one activities.

The following sections provide general strategies or formats for practice that are referenced by the lesson plans.

DISABLED LEARNERS

A learning-disabled student has special needs due to poorly developed reading, organization, concentration, or task-analysis skills. Some of these students learn better through visual means, others through auditory means. Some students have trouble working independently, in which case one-to-one feedback and smaller tasks are helpful.

Become attuned to your students' learning styles. Do they appear restless when the teaching is primarily oral? Or do they need verbal explanations? Teaching to the way each student learns best can be facilitated by the activities in this section geared to auditory, visual, and dependent learners.

The chart on pages 112–113 provides general formats for activities grounded in the *strengths* of disabled learners. Specific activities in the lesson plans are keyed to these general formats.

SPANISH-SPEAKING LEARNERS

The *Ginn English Program* is designed for use with students whose primary language for learning is English. The program recognizes, however, that many classrooms have sizable Spanish-speaking populations. The Spanish-speaking bilingual student is one who needs to know English in school, yet who speaks Spanish at home.

Thus, specific lesson-plan activities—oral and written drills—are suggested that focus on concepts in the English language that may be troublesome to the Spanish-bilingual student. Included are notes pointing out errors that are common to bilingual students.

The chart to the left provides general formats for pattern practice suggested in the lesson plans.

PATTERN PRACTICE FOR SPANISH-SPEAKING LEARNERS

Repetition
Give a sentence for students to repeat verbatim. Then change the part of the sentence that is being drilled and have students repeat the new sentence.

Substitution
Give a sentence. Students replace the target word, make any corresponding changes (e.g., a noun being made plural requires a verb change as well), and respond with the new sentence.

Question-Answer
Ask a question to which the student responds with a sentence that uses the target skill. Or, give a sentence for students to change into a question.

This format is sometimes expanded such that you ask a question for which the answer requires a substitution of the target word.

Example-Response
Indicate people or objects to be used and label them. (E.g., for pronouns, point to two students and say, "They, them.") Then give a sentence and point to the people or objects indicated by the target word. ("['mmm'] are in class.") Students make a new sentence by changing the target word. ("They are in class.")

SPEAKERS OF NONSTANDARD ENGLISH

A standard variety of English is one that is widely accepted as a model. It includes both formal and informal English, where the formal is the type used in serious writing (research papers, essays, etc.) and the informal is the type used in magazines, public speeches, and so on. Nonstandard English is any dialect or usage style that is used by a smaller overall group than is true for standard English.

A dialect has its own pronunciation and grammar system that may interfere when students attempt to learn standard English. The areas of interference are called *conflict points*. Some examples of conflict points are—

- omission of the agreement sound represented by the /s/ at the end of third-person singular, present tense verbs;

- different forms of the verb *be;*

- use of object pronouns as subjects;

- use of double or multiple negatives.

Nonstandard dialect features are not "errors" made by individual children; rather, they are features of a spoken dialect and will be applied consistently by all speakers of that dialect. That is, dialect speakers as a group will always make similar substitutions for the standard English features. These children need to learn that school is where they learn another variety of English—an *alternate* dialect—to use in appropriate situations.

The chart to the right presents a general teaching strategy to follow with each lesson that contains a conflict point. The lesson plans state the specific conflict points.

FOUR-STEP STRATEGY FOR SPEAKERS OF NONSTANDARD ENGLISH

Note: Conduct steps 1 and 2 before or early in the regular Lesson Steps. Use of the tape recorder is recommended to help students learn to hear standard English sounds and patterns. Remember that it is essential to establish usage patterns orally.

1. **Contrasting the standard and nonstandard features**
   Explain that the lesson contains a feature that may not be used in the students' "everyday" language. Do not imply that the standard feature is "good" and the nonstandard "bad." They are simply different.

   Give paired examples of the standard feature and the nonstandard feature in sentences. ("The horse paws the ground. The horse paw the ground.") Give the examples both orally and in writing.

2. **Discriminating between the features**
   Orally present nonpaired sentences containing the standard feature and the nonstandard feature. ("I and he left early. Jennifer and she went swimming.") Have students identify which sentences contain which feature. Have students repeat the standard-feature sentence.

3. **Using pattern practice and drill**
   Give both oral and written drills on using the standard feature. Do the oral drills as a group activity.

   Provide exercises that have students translate nonstandard usage into standard usage.

4. **Using the standard feature**
   Have students use the standard feature in their speech. This may be done by—

   - having students give original sentences containing the standard feature;

   - simulating situations in which standard English should be used (talking with a librarian, for example);

   - selecting a standard feature for the class to focus on and use throughout the day.

Helping Atypical Learners

GENERAL FORMATS FOR DISABLED LEARNERS

AUDITORY LEARNERS
(learn best through listening)

VISUAL LEARNERS
(learn best through seeing)

A-1. TAPE RECORDER

Tape-record stories, songs, poems, and other instructional material so that auditory learners may have the benefit of many individual repetitions to learn the material.

Place a self-adhesive green dot on the "Play" button, a red dot on the "Stop" button, and a white dot with an "R" on it on the "Rewind" button. Put only one piece of instructional material on each tape to avoid difficulties finding where one piece ends and another begins.

A-2. DIALOGUE

A concept can often be learned or practiced by two people asking and answering questions of each other.

A-2a. Student-Pair Dialogue: A disabled student may be paired with a second student (disabled or not) with both students profiting. Brief questions and answers, with silence in between for thinking, can be effective following group lessons to identify misunderstandings and to clarify application of the concepts.

A-2b. Teacher-Student Dialogue: While students are doing practice items, move from student to student or pair to pair. Allowing students to do most of the talking, pinpoint those who have mastered the concept, those who may benefit from *Student-Pair Dialogue* (A-2a), and those who will need further help from you.

V-1. MODEL T

Visual learners often need to see someone doing what they are to do, or see a finished copy of what they are to produce.

While showing visual learners how to do something, remember it is difficult for some children to transpose right and left hand when facing you. Let them watch you from behind, over your shoulder, or as you stand behind them with your arms around in front of them.

Use traditional tracing and "copy me" techniques and use many gestures when you explain things orally.

V-2. PICTURE THIS

Many students need training to draw with their "mind's eye" the concept they are learning. Present the concept as an exaggerated mind-picture, appealing to as many senses as possible to develop a strong visual image. This taps the visual learner's strength; it also helps the auditory learner to picture what is heard.

Prepare students by saying,
"Relax . . . Close your eyes . . . Erase the chalkboard in your mind so that it is totally blank. . . ."

Then read the group lesson and follow it with a dialogue format (A-2a or 2b).

V-3. TEACHER FLOAT

While students work independently or in pairs, move among them to give quick suggestions for corrections without providing answers. Make as many stops as possible in a short period of time. If you tell a student to correct a sentence, for example, move on and return in a short while to check it. This deskside technique is more brisk and uses less conversation than *Teacher-Student Dialogue* (A-2b).

DEPENDENT LEARNERS
(learn best through interaction or small tasks)

D-1. YES-NO QUESTIONS

Ask yes-no questions to check understanding of a concept, rewording the concept in many ways. Ask: "Does this mean that . . ." and "Could we also say that . . .," calling on one student, a student pair, or the whole group. Use "yes" and "no" response cards colored green (yes) and red (no).

D-2. PLAY-OFF

Play a game with the entire class for a limited time period. Have students perform a specified task (described in the individual lesson plans). Those students who respond correctly continue to play the game; those who respond incorrectly are out of the game. The students still in the game at the end of the time period are winners.

D-3. Class Examples

Do several examples as a class. Use chalkboard or overhead transparencies. Involve students by having them do the examples and by using their personal experiences. For example, the names of dependent learners might be used when illustrating proper nouns.

D-4. FINE-MOTOR SOS

Many students may have difficulty using the muscles needed to do fine-motor tasks, such as writing or using scissors. Some students will need supervision or help during these tasks. With scissors or pencils, provide various kinds, as one type may be easier to use than another. Allow students to practice writing large letters on the chalkboard.

Vocabulary Teaching Strategies

Specific activities for teaching the instructional vocabulary are provided in the individual lesson plans. This section provides additional activities that may be used with certain types of oral vocabulary as well as further suggestions for teaching the instructional vocabulary.

INSTRUCTIONAL VOCABULARY

Instructional terms are words you might not expect students to know yet, but whose meanings they need to know in order to do the tasks. These words include concept and directive terms, such as *square* and *mark an X,* and directional terms, such as *above* and *first.*

Introducing a Term: Say the term and its definition. Give several examples of the term and ask students to suggest others. For instance, say: "Red. *Red* is a color." (Show a red object.) "Can you tell me something else that is red?" (Students may point out red objects in the classroom or they may suggest any item they know to be red.)

"Guess My Word": Place some objects on a table or desk. Ask students to tell where a specific object is as you point to it. (Example: "The pencil is to the left of the book.") Encourage the use of the appropriate directional words. This activity may also be used for words such as *first, next, last.*

ORAL VOCABULARY

These words are primarily from the songs, stories, and poems that are read to students. Although the meanings of some words may be unfamiliar to students, generally students do not need to know the word meanings in order to complete the text activity. You may wish to employ the following strategies, however, in order to increase oral vocabulary.

Context: By using context clues, have students guess what a word might mean. For example, with the song "A Little Boy Went Walking," you might ask: "If a river is *winding* in and out, what do you think it is doing?" (changing direction, turning, not straight)

Example: Examples which clarify word meaning may be given in several ways. For the word *creeping,* you may ask for or tell students another word that means almost the same thing. *(crawling)* You may have students demonstrate what the word means by performing the action. (Students "creep" on the floor.) With other words you may wish to explain word meaning by giving opposite examples. *(obey—disobey)*

Definition: Some words will require defining. For example, *curds* and *whey* in "Little Miss Muffet" would need to be defined in simple terms. ("thick milk" and "watery milk" or "two kinds of milk")

Visualization: Many of the oral vocabulary words are pictured in the text. Use the text illustrations as a means of defining the words. Say the word: "Octopus." Then point out the illustration in the text. Say: "This is an octopus." You may wish to tell more about the word but usually this is not necessary.

GRADE K WORD LIST

Instructional Vocabulary

above
alike
alphabet
back
behind
below
big
black
blue
bottom
brown
capital letter
circle
different
down
first
fourth
front
in front of
inside
last
left
little
"mark an X"
medium
middle
next
outside
over
purple
rectangle
red
right
row
rows
second

sentence
small letter
square
then
third
top
triangle
under
up
white

Oral Vocabulary

angry
answer
balance
bank
blackberry
book title
bouquet
briefcase
broad bill
bulldozer
bureau
cabbage
cape
carpenter
checkout counter
church steeple
circus
clerk
connect
cottage
country
cover
creeping
cucumber
curds
dash
disobey
dormouse
elf
eggshell
elbow pads
engine
eye doctor
factory
fan

favorite
feathery
fiddlers
fire alarm
fire hydrant
fluffy
frame
fruit
furiously
gooseberry
gracious
gray
groceries
gym
hatch
heap
helmet
hoarse
hoe
hood
iguana
invent
journey
knee pads
lament
lion tamer
map
mill
mischief
naughty
nibble
octopus
owl
parsley
peck
plumber
pointed beak
pompom

porcupine
prickly hair
rooster
safety
scarecrow
scatter
scoop
scramble
shelter
silky
siren
skyscraper
sparrow
sprawl
stubby
stung
sunflower seeds
surprised
tennis racket
The End
tire swing
toadstool
tool shed
topple
trapped
tuffet
tug
tumble
underbrush
uniform
United States
vacuum cleaner
valentine
vegetable
velvet
vine

waddle
wand
wasp
web
week
whey
whisker
winding
wood
worm

Letter 1 from the Teacher

Dear

Your child will be using the *Ginn English Program, Grade K* this year. This program builds listening and speaking skills. It also teaches skills that will be important as your child learns to read and write.

In the first part of the book, students will listen to and talk about stories, poems, and nursery rhymes. They will follow directions and learn about colors and shapes.

You can help your child at home. Here are some activities to choose from:

- Give each other directions to follow, such as "Raise your left hand" and "Blink three times."
- Point out and talk about objects that have these shapes: circle, square, rectangle, and triangle. These objects might include signs, crackers, buildings, and dishes.
- Have your child tell about the colors of things he or she sees.
- Read together. Talk about the stories and poems you read.
- Go to the public library to read and check out books.

I look forward to working with your child this year. Please feel free to call me with any comments or suggestions about your child's work.

Sincerely,

Letter 2 from the Teacher

Dear

The class has finished the first unit of the *Ginn English Program, Grade K*. Students have heard and talked about stories and poems. They have talked about how objects are alike and how they are different.

In the next unit, students will begin to sort objects according to size—big, medium, and little. They will also sort objects by how they are used. Students will retell in the correct order stories that they hear.

Here are some activities that you and your child might try at home:

- Sort objects by size or by color.
- Have your child match socks. Talk about how the objects are alike (all are socks) and how they are different (they are different colors).
- Have your child sort or put away silverware, keeping the knives, forks, and spoons separate. Talk about how the objects are alike and different.
- Read stories and ask your child to tell what happens in the beginning, middle, and end.
- If your public library has a story hour, arrange for your child to attend.

Please feel free to call with any comments or suggestions about your child's work.

Sincerely,

Letter 3 from the Teacher

Dear

Your child has finished the second unit of the *Ginn English Program, Grade K*. The class has been listening to stories and poems, telling stories in order, and learning new words.

The last unit teaches capital and small letters. Students will continue listening to stories and poems and talking about activities. Here are some activities you might try at home:

- Have your child point out and name letters he or she recognizes.
- Make a game of pointing to a capital letter in a newspaper or magazine and having your child find the matching small letter.
- Keep reading and talking about stories and poems. Try reading a part of a story and asking what might happen next.
- Have your child give a puppet show about a story you have read. Puppets can be made by drawing on light-colored socks with crayons or markers.

Please feel free to call me. I welcome any questions or suggestions you have about your child's work.

Sincerely,

Index

READING SERVICE

Notes

Notes

Notes

Notes

Notes

Notes

Notes